My Diary: Emily Owen

GW00535701

Authentic

Text copyright © 2021 Emily Owen
Illustrations copyright © 2021 Beatriz Albano

27 26 25 24 23 22 21   7 6 5 4 3 2 1

First published 2021 by Authentic Media Limited,
PO Box 6326, Bletchley, Milton Keynes, MK1 9GG.
authenticmedia.co.uk

British Library Cataloguing in Publication Data
A catalogue record for this book is available from the British Library.
ISBN: 978-1-78893-166-3
978-1-78893-167-0 (e-book)

Unless otherwise noted, Scriptures are quoted from the
International Children's Bible, New Century Version (Anglicised Edition)
copyright © 1991 by Authentic. Used by permission.

'I know that my redeemer liveth' is from
The Authorized (King James) Version.
Rights in the Authorized Version in the United Kingdom
are vested in the Crown. Reproduced by permission
of the Crown's patentee, Cambridge University Press.

Some names have been changed.

Cover design by Beatriz Albano
Printed and bound by CPI Group (UK) Ltd, Croydon, CR0 4YY

*This diary is about real life.
Sometimes sad things happen.*

1993

Nightmare!

Nightmare! Mum wants me to keep a diary and write down things that happen in my life. What a silly idea – I don't really have anything to write. My life's fine, but it's not exactly exciting. Interesting stuff doesn't happen to me, but I promised Mum I'd try, so I will. Here goes . . .

I feel so stupid

My chin hurts. It's so boring, sitting here on blue plastic chairs in the hospital waiting room. Yes, I did say hospital, and all because I fell off the trampoline in gymnastics, in front of everyone, and I landed on my chin. There was blood everywhere, all over the floor of the gym and dripping onto my leotard, so the teacher sent me to hospital. What's worse than being at the hospital? Being at the hospital in a leotard. With a plaster on my chin. What a great look – not.

I need to see a doctor and get my chin sewn up. Here we go again . . .

But I suppose I should start at the beginning and explain who I am. I'm only telling you, though.

It's alright if you read my diary, but I don't want anyone else to see it, OK?

This is me

I am Emily. Thirteen years old. Tall, skinny, knobbly knees. I got called 'Mummy Longlegs' at junior school, which I hated but pretended I didn't mind. I've got three little sisters, who are fine – most of the time. Sometimes they really wind me up, though! They're called Sophie, Kirsty and Pollyanna.

I like running, and hockey, and any sport, really, except football. And except gymnastics now.

I'm good at English but rubbish at maths. I like music; I play the flute and the piano. I go to church (I used to get bullied for that). My family don't have a TV. I don't mind that – I prefer reading books anyway – but people think it's weird. I used to get bullied for that as well. People can be really mean.

I have some nice friends. I like my life, except for the bullies, and except when it means I have to be in hospital in the Accident and Emergency department (A&E), like now. I hope they call my name to see the doctor soon. I just want to get out of here.

Three stitches

I've got three stitches on my chin. They're called butterfly stitches. I have no idea why they're called that; butterflies are nice, aren't they, but these stitches aren't. They itch, not to mention looking a bit silly. White plasters on my chin. I didn't like the butterfly name the first time, either . . . which reminds me: I need to tell you why I said 'Here we go again . . .'.

When I was 11, I was skipping, trying to do 100 skips as fast as I could. I got to number 67, and then . . . Well, OK, it might not have been exactly 67, but it was about that. Anyway, the skipping rope tangled in my feet, and I fell over and landed on my chin. Can you guess what's coming? Blood, hospital, blue plastic chairs, doctor, butterfly stitches. The only difference was that it was a trampoline not a skipping rope that did it today. Oh, and the skipping rope time I was not wearing a leotard.

Egg sandwiches

Stitches on my chin and bruises, but do I get a day off school? No way. My mum would probably need me to have my arm chopped off before she'd think about letting me have a day off. She gave me egg sandwiches for my lunch today, though, so I think she does feel a bit sorry for me!

I walk to school with some of my friends. One sets off, then calls for another on the way, and so it goes on. I'm the third one to be called for, and by the time we get to school there are four of us.

Recently, the others have been laughing and saying I walk further than them, even though I live second nearest to school. I laugh about it, too, and they're right! The thing is, I can't seem to walk in a straight line. When I walk with them, they walk straight, but I wobble from side to side. I can't remember when that started, but it's become so normal now, it doesn't really bother me. Do you think it's OK not to be able to walk straight?

It would bother me if I couldn't run, but when I run I don't wobble. Weird, isn't it?!

Good thing, really, because I run in lots of races. I don't normally win, but I often come second or third. I love running.

Duets

The doctor took the stitches off and said my chin is healing up well. I still feel stupid about the whole thing – well, wouldn't you feel a bit stupid?! – but now at least I won't be reminded about it every time I look in a mirror.

Or every time I play my flute. Have you ever tried playing a flute with bruises on your chin? It really hurts, but it's still better than not playing. Music is my world. I'm practising duets with my sister at the moment. Duet means where two people play music together. Sophie plays clarinet, and I play flute. Duets don't really work if one person doesn't play, and anyway, I love making music. At least my chin didn't make it harder to play the piano, though now I think of it, I should have used it as an excuse! When I have my piano lesson, my teacher always seems to know I haven't practised. I love playing the piano, but I don't like practising the same old exercises again and again, so I don't, but she always seems to know! I should have thought to say I couldn't practise because of my chin. I don't think she'd have believed me. Ha ha!

But I really like my teacher; she's great. And at the end of the lesson, she always stays a bit longer to play duets with me.

No sand in my shoes!

Soon it'll be time for me to run the 800m race for my school. That means twice round the track. I'm glad I was picked for 800m, it's my best distance. I'm doing stretches now, to warm up ready for the race. When I turn my head to loosen up my neck muscles, I can see the sandpit. I'm glad I don't have to do the long jump and land in the sand and get sand in my shoes. I hate getting sand in my shoes.

I saw you jump

I have got sand in my shoes now. Don't laugh! The person who should have done the long jump was ill, and when the teacher asked me to jump instead, there was no question I'd do it. This is sport!

What's amazing is that I came in second, even though I've hardly ever tried the long jump. I still couldn't wait to get the sand out of my shoes, though! As I walked away from the sandpit with my dad, who always watches me doing sport, a man came up to us. He was wearing a tracksuit, and he looked really sporty. He said, 'Hi, I saw you jump. You're good. I want you to join my athletics club.' I thought he was joking, or maybe talking to someone behind me, but when I turned round, there was no one there. He *was* talking to me. I looked at Dad. Then I looked back at the man, and I asked him what it would involve. He said, 'Coming every Sunday and training with the club.'

God or sport?

Oh. You know I said before that I go to church? I go on Sundays. I've never not wanted to go. Well, nearly never. There was one time, when I was maybe 11, when I decided I wasn't going to church any more. People at school didn't go, so why should I? I knew it wouldn't go down well with my parents, but I was old enough to make my own decisions. I told Mum firmly one Sunday morning that I was not going to church with the rest of them, and I would just stay at home. Well, I thought I said it firmly, but Mum didn't! She said, 'Of course you're coming with us, get in the car.' And that was that, I got in the car. I sat there, feeling really mad that I had to be there, and trying to think how I could make sure everyone in the car knew. In the end, I announced, in my crossest voice, 'Just so you know, my body is here, but I'm not.' Then I turned away from them all and stared out of the window. That'll show them, I thought. Then I heard Mum laughing! Can you believe it? She thought I'd said something funny. Anyway, in the end, I calmed down, remembered I like church, and I love God, and that was the end of my 'rebellion'. Church was, and still is, a big part of my life.

So there I am, standing with sand in my shoes, and there's a man in a tracksuit asking me to join his club. It felt like I was being asked to choose between God and sport.

Both things I love. But it didn't take me long to choose. I love God more than anything, even sport. So I said no to the athletics club.

I also decided to get baptized, to show that God comes first in my life, and I want to follow him. Here's a top tip: if you get baptized by full immersion like I did, do not wear a skirt. I wore a skirt and as I went down into the water, my skirt floated to the top!

Broken glass

I said no to long jump, but I didn't say no to running. Every Saturday in winter, my friend Katie calls for me, and we go and race for our school. We love cross-country running! Except today didn't work out as planned.

Katie rang the doorbell, which was fine. I heard it and went to answer it, which was fine. What wasn't fine was the thing that happened next. There is a mat on the floor near the door; my mum says it's to protect the carpet, but I don't know why the carpet needs protecting.

Today, I tripped on the mat, put out my hand to stop me falling, and my hand reached the door. The door has lots of glass in it, and you can probably guess what happened next! Imagine it from Katie's point of view:

She rings the bell, and waits for the door to open. Instead of the door opening, she sees a hand – my hand – break through the glass and move towards her. Oh, and my hand was dripping blood.

It was like something out of a horror movie. No wonder Katie screamed and ran home! It's a good thing she only lives across the road.

I think my mum heard her scream. Or maybe I screamed, too; I don't know. Anyway, Mum came, saw what had happened, ran to the kitchen, grabbed a towel and came and wrapped it round my wrist (most of the blood was coming from my wrist). Then Mum wrapped her hands tightly round the towel and held my arm up as high as she could. I found out later that helps slow the bleeding down, but at the time all I could think about was that it hurt.

Mum yelled for Dad to come, sent my sisters over to Katie's house and shoved me into the car – still squeezing my wrist and holding my arm in the air – and Dad drove us to the hospital as fast as he could.

So, right now, I'm sitting on a blue plastic chair. Again! No prizes for guessing where I am. My wrist and hand have a bandage now, not a towel. At least it's my left hand, so I can still write this and tell you what's happening. A doctor put the bandage on, but now I need to see another doctor. When the first one looked at my wrist, I looked at it too, and it does look bad; I can see why Katie screamed. There's this big cut on the side, just below my hand. You can see right in, right down to the tendon. The tendon is white, and I thought it was bone, but the doctor told me it's a tendon. Then he got some tweezers and pulled at the tendon. When he pulled it, my little finger moved. I was nearly sick! It's really weird seeing my finger move when I didn't move it. Eugh.

Stay

I'm home now. So relieved. They nearly didn't let me come home! When I saw the second doctor, he looked at my wrist and then said I'd need to stay in hospital tonight and have an operation tomorrow. Stay in hospital? I can't think of anything worse. Don't tell anyone, but I started to cry. I'm a bit embarrassed about that, but I was so scared. The doctor felt sorry for me and had another look at my wrist, then said he'd sew it up right away, and I could go home. He's the best doctor ever. He sewed the cut up, then put a massive bandage on, and I came home.

You know what? I think this is going to be worse than my chin. No piano or flute. No running, in case I fall and damage my wrist more. At least I can still read.

Mum's serious voice

Had my bandage taken off a few weeks ago and my hand is fine. Now if my little finger moves it's because I move it, not because a doctor pulls a bone-that's-actually-tendon.

I can play the flute and piano again, and run. I can even play the guitar. Did I tell you that I'm learning guitar?

So that's all fine, but something's not. Yesterday, Mum said she wanted to talk to me, and she said it in that serious voice she saves for important things. She wants to take me to see the doctor. Like I've not had enough of blue plastic chairs and doctors. It's because I can't walk in a straight line, and I keep falling over. And because of the headache. I don't really talk about it, but I have a headache all the time.

So we're going to see the doctor next week. Not the doctor I saw in hospital – this one is my GP. He's known me since I was 5.

What a headache

I sat there while mum explained to Dr Allen what was wrong. Well, I told him as well. He seemed to agree with what I think, it's the permanent headache that's the problem; the walking wobbly and falling over is just me. The doctor gave me tablets for migraine. I don't know much about migraines, do you? I read that they make people need to lie down in the dark. I've never had to do that, but hopefully these tablets will help. Granny has bad headaches and we all have to be really quiet when she's here.

Tablets

I took the tablets for weeks and weeks, but they didn't help, so I went back to the doctor and got different migraine tablets.

1995

Falling over

Today I fell over in a cave. Yes, you did read that correctly! I'm in Wales with school and today we went caving. It was fine until it got so dark I couldn't see anything, which is when I fell over. My teacher had to come back and find me, then lead me out. I felt a bit – OK, very – silly but, once I could see, I was OK.

I think I'll try to forget about the cave. Will you try to forget it, too?!

Not helping

Tablets still not helping. I've got different ones from the doctor.

New tablets

The new tablets are not helping and my headache is just getting worse. I went back to see Dr Allen, who said the headache is maybe because I'm stressed with preparing for my exams. I managed not to laugh! Exams do not stress me out. I've never minded them (apart from maths, obviously). Anyway, Dr Allen gave me different tablets. Hopefully these ones will help. Exams don't stress me, but the headache does make it hard to concentrate.

No more school!

Exams are over. Headache is not over, but I'm learning to ignore it, which is weird since it's getting worse, but anyway, I've got bigger worries right now. Exams over means end of school. Well, end of this school. And end of school means School Leavers' Dinner. If ever I have wished I was cool, it's now! No idea what to wear. I kind of don't want to go, but my mum says I should go, because I'm head girl. I suppose she's right, really.

At the beginning of exam year, head girl and head boy are chosen from the top year group. Everyone in the year group votes for who they want, and I couldn't believe it when I got the most votes and ended up being head girl!

Dancing

The dinner was OK; I just wore a black dress in the end. Afterwards, everyone except me went clubbing. Here's a secret: I have never been clubbing in my life. There. I said it. I don't like the thumping music, and I can't dance. Well, I can do ballroom dancing, but that's different. I know what to do in ballroom dancing, I learn the moves and steps, but I can't do just standing and jigging about!

I am quite good at ballroom dancing. I've passed exams and won prizes. There's this one step, called 'The Fan', that I used to be able to do but can't now. It's where you move along the dance floor one foot in front of the other really close, like heel to toe.

I don't know why I can't do it now, but it doesn't matter because I don't need it for most dances anyway. So the others went clubbing and I went home. School is over! Until I start Sixth Form after the summer, anyway.

Tablet update

Tablets are still not helping. Dr Allen gave me some different ones.

Red shorts

I went on beach mission this summer. I went last year as well. Do you know what beach mission is? It's where you help run a children's club on the beach and tell them stories from the Bible, and about Jesus, and play games. It's really fun. Except I had to wear red shorts and a white top, because it's the uniform. I don't like shorts and before I did beach mission, I definitely didn't own any red ones, so Mum and I looked in charity shops to find some I could wear. At beach mission, we teach the children songs, and they love it. I played the accordion for the singing this time. Accordion is a bit like playing the piano, so it didn't take me long to learn – which is a good thing, really, because I had to learn overnight. There was no one else to play! But I like playing, so it was OK.

Life is good

I started sixth form college. None of my friends from my old school goes to the same college as me but that's OK, and I'll still see Jodie at church and youth group. This is the first time Jo and I have not been at the same school since we were 5! We met on our first day at primary school. She's my best friend.

I'm taking four A levels: English literature, French, psychology and music. I chose them because they are my favourite subjects, except for psychology; I've never studied psychology before, but I think it'll be interesting.

So I'm at a different college, and it's all new, but the headache and balance and stuff is not better. I still have to keep trying different tablets. I'm not letting it stop me, though. I joined the hockey team at college and a county orchestra playing flute, and I'm making friends. Only one or two, which is fine, because I don't really like crowds. Everything is good.

Thump thump thump

I didn't go to college today. Mum said enough is enough. I don't mean enough lessons and studying, she'd never say that! She wants me to do well. I mean about the headache. This morning, my headache was really bad, but I didn't tell anyone. I 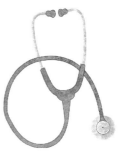 don't really talk about it. I mean, if I have pain, and then I talk about my pain, it will make the pain worse, don't you think?

So I try to ignore it. I've had lots of practise at ignoring it over the last two years, but it's getting harder and harder to ignore. The tablets make no difference, they're a waste of space. This morning, as I was getting my coat, ready to walk to college, it was suddenly like my head exploded, the pain was so bad. Without even thinking, I left my coat on the peg and lay down on the floor, and that's where Mum found me, banging my head against the floor. Thump, thump, thump. Mum said, 'Emily, what are you doing?' Thump, thump.

Thump. I said 'I'm – *thump* – trying – *thump* – to – *thump* – bang the – *thump* – headache – *thump* – out – *thump* – of my – *thump* – head.'

Mum picked up the phone right then and called the doctor. I got an appointment with him the same day. Today. This afternoon. I don't know how many different tablets Dr Allen has given me to try over the last months, but today he said no more, and he's going to send me to the neurology department at the hospital. I've heard of neurology. When Granny was in hospital a few years ago, she was on the neurology ward. She was there at Christmas and was sad that she would not be with the rest of the family on Christmas Day, so we all visited her instead and – get this – my sisters and I had to sing for her, in front of all the other patients. We felt a bit embarrassed, but Granny loved it, and so did the other patients.

I'm used to singing and playing music with my sisters, we do it a lot, but normally at home, not in a hospital!

Anyway, that's my only experience of neurology. Hopefully when I go for myself, the doctor there will know a tablet to stop my headaches. It won't be for ages yet, though. Everyone says you have to wait a loooooong time to get an appointment at the hospital.

What waiting?

I've got an appointment for next week! So much for having to wait a long time. When Mum and I got home from seeing Dr Allen, we'd hardly got through the door when the phone rang.

It was Dr Allen, telling us I have an appointment already. I don't know why people say it's hard to get appointments! I have an appointment for next week, and it's not as though there is even anything seriously wrong with me. The headaches are annoying, and they do hurt, but I'm OK.

Neurology

Neurology clinic is not the same place as I visited Granny. It's in the same building as the blue plastic chairs in A&E, but here the chairs are green. They are comfier as well; the blue ones gave me a numb bum! And at least I'm not sitting here in a leotard. I've got my schoolbooks in my bag because as soon as the doctor has given me the tablets that will help, I'm going to college. I don't want to miss my English lesson, so I hope the doctor is quick.

Failing

The doctor was not quick. She took ages. When I went into her room and sat down, I said, 'I've got headaches.' She said, 'Can you straighten your arm, then bend your elbow and touch your nose with your finger?' I was thinking, what? Of course I can. So I showed her, and I couldn't believe it: I can *not* touch my nose with my finger. Repeat; can *not*. I tried and tried but I just kept missing my nose. Then the doctor asked if I could walk – not dance – across the room with one foot in front of the other, heel to toe. Of course I could. So I showed her. And I fell over! Actually fell over! She gave me more things to do, and I couldn't do any of them. I hated that. I'm not used to failing tests. After about half an hour of failing tests – fun, hey? – the doctor said she was going to get the consultant to see me. Consultant means the top doctor. Brilliant; if anyone knows the tablets to give me, he will. Everyone but me seems to have forgotten that I'm here to get headache tablets. I said to Mum that it's great I'm seeing the top doctor, but she didn't reply, so I don't know if she agreed with me. When the doctor arrived, the first thing I noticed was that he had Disney characters on his tie. I liked that, but then he made me do all the same tests again. Can you touch your nose? No. Can you walk heel to toe? No. Etc. For another half hour.

I don't think I'm going to get to English.

Dr Disney

It turned out not only was I not going to English, but I was not even allowed to leave the hospital. Dr Disney said he wanted to get photos – or scans – of my brain. I still don't know why he can't just give me tablets to make me better, but maybe the scans will tell him which ones to give me.

So here I am, lying in a hospital bed, waiting for my scan time. The scariest thing just happened. There are six beds in my room, three each side, and I'm in the first bed on the right-hand side as you go in. Diagonally opposite me, in the middle bed on the other side, is an old lady. When I saw her, I was surprised because she looked really poorly. I'm in hospital, and I don't feel poorly. But she just kept turning greyer and greyer. I was worried about her and I said to Mum, 'That lady looks really ill.' Then doctors and nurses were running to her bed. They pulled these blue, patterned curtains round it, and I couldn't see what was happening. The next thing I knew, the curtains were pulled back and the lady was wheeled away in her bed, with a sheet covering her. I knew that meant she'd died.

I'm only 16! I'm supposed to be in my English lesson. But instead I'm in hospital, watching people die. Can you believe it? So, if people die in hospital, and I'm in hospital, even I can do that maths. People do not leave here alive. I only came to get headache tablets.

Gingerbread man

It's time for my scans. I know that because someone has just arrived to take me. They said I have to go in a wheelchair. A wheelchair! What's going on? I can walk! I'm fine! I just need tablets. Why doesn't anyone understand that?

I'm glad Mum is with me.

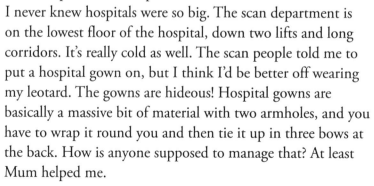

The wheelchair took me to a different part of the hospital. I never knew hospitals were so big. The scan department is on the lowest floor of the hospital, down two lifts and long corridors. It's really cold as well. The scan people told me to put a hospital gown on, but I think I'd be better off wearing my leotard. The gowns are hideous! Hospital gowns are basically a massive bit of material with two armholes, and you have to wrap it round you and then tie it up in three bows at the back. How is anyone supposed to manage that? At least Mum helped me.

I got to the door of the room where the machine is, and I stopped. I could see the machine. It looked like a tunnel, and

I realized I was going to have to lie in it. I was really scared by that. I'm supposed to be in my English lesson! Well, not now, I'd probably be in my flute lesson by now, but you get the point. I've just failed lots of tests, been told I need pictures of my brain, seen someone die, and now I have to lie in a tunnel so small the top of it will nearly touch my nose. None of this is normal. Even I don't blame me for being scared.

I told the hospital person that I was not going in. They said I had to. I said, 'Well, I'm not going in on my own.' They said I had to. No one else would fit in the tunnel with me anyway, it's so small. But they said my mum could come in the room. It was scary in the tunnel. I was in there for more than an hour, and I couldn't move or even see out, like a gingerbread man in an oven. My feet were sticking out of the end of the tunnel, though. If my feet had eyes on, I'd have been OK! But I felt Mum's hand on my foot the whole time. It made me feel a bit less scared.

Not a joke

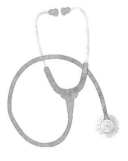

While I was in the scan, Dad arrived at the hospital. He's a teacher. He teaches maths. I definitely don't share his ability with numbers, which my maths teachers all assume I should. Mum phoned Dad at work before my scan, and he came to hospital in his lunch break. He got here just in time to go back up to the ward with us after my scan. I'm on a different ward now, it's not the one where I saw the lady die. The scan was a nightmare, by the way. I never want to have to go through that again, lying in a narrow tunnel for ages, and I couldn't move or see out. Plus there was a noise like a road drill going all the time. I just hope the scan showed up what tablets I need. I walked back to the ward: I've no idea why they think having a scan means I don't need a wheelchair (that I didn't need in the first place). When Mum, Dad and I got to my hospital bed, there was a crowd of doctors standing round it. 'How many people does it take to tell me what tablets I need?' I thought. I smiled at that; it sounds like a joke! The doctors were waiting for us. It was a bit confusing seeing all these people – I couldn't even see my bed there were so many – but then I spotted a tie with Disney characters all over it. At least I recognized someone in the crowd. Dr Disney told me to lie on the bed, so I did. I felt really small, lying there looking up at them all. I never feel small! I'm always one of the tallest people in a group. I focused on the Disney characters. Dr Disney said, 'You've got two brain tumours in your head, and they're so big they are about to kill you.' How many doctors does it take to . . . I'm not smiling now. What? Brain tumours? I stared at the Disney tie. Words drifted to me: 'Not cancer', 'Stay in hospital', 'Neurofibromatosis Type 2' (NF2), 'Surgery'. Then, Dr Disney and the rest were gone. Mum sat down. Dad looked like he was going to faint. I don't even know how I felt, but I know I was hungry. Dad handed me his packed lunch. He didn't want it. I've never known Dad not eat.

I bent my head and bit into a sandwich. I don't think tablets are going to fix this.

Brain surgery

Tablets aren't going to fix it, but they are going to get me ready for surgery. Brain surgery. Dr Disney says my tumours are not safe to operate on, so I need to take tablets called steroids to make them safe. The tumours are also too big to let me go home. Remember Dr Disney said they were about to kill me? That's because the tumours are so big that they are squashing my brainstem, which is where all the nerves from my brain go to make my body work. I'm glad the tumours are not cancer. I have to stay in hospital, in the bed nearest the nurses' desk, so they can keep an eye on me. It does feel weird to be in hospital. The other people on my ward are really poorly; some of them can't move at all, but I can move fine. I feel bad that I'm in the bed for the most ill patient. I'm not ill. I feel exactly the same as I did before I came into hospital. Dad's gone back to work now, and Mum has gone home to get my pyjamas. I'm on my own.

Brave

I'm trying to be brave.

Home

I wish I could have gone home with Mum. I'm glad she will be back soon with my pyjamas.

Can't sleep

Sleeping in hospital is impossible, even with my own pyjamas, not a hospital gown. It's so noisy at night with nurses coming and going, and people calling out. And then there's the lights. I like it to be really dark when I sleep, but here the lights are always on. I woke up really early – if I'd been to sleep at all – which was good because Dr Disney came to see me first thing in the morning. He didn't say much, just checked I was taking my steroids, but he was wearing the Disney tie again. That cheered me up a bit. And then I felt even better because Mum arrived. She'd taken my sisters to school and then come to the hospital. I smelled her perfume. She smelled like Mum always smells. I felt like things would be OK.

Chocolate Buttons

The only way people can contact me in hospital is if they phone the ward and whoever answers the phone at the nurses' desk comes and tells me. Or if they come to visit, but that's only allowed for two hours in the afternoon and two hours in the evening. There's a nurse on the ward called Clare. I really like her. She sends most people away after the two hours, so the patients don't get too tired, but she lets Mum stay as long as Mum wants to. Maybe Mum doesn't count as a visitor.

Mum and I were sitting by my bed on the main ward, where we'd been sitting all morning – there's nothing else to do – and

Clare came over. I think she realizes I feel a bit lost. If this brain tumour thing had happened a year ago, I'd have been on the children's ward, with toys and games. As it is, because I'm 16, I'm on an adult ward, surrounded by people older than me (some of them *much* older), who are really poorly, and I feel fine. But I'm in the emergency bed. It's strange. And not in a good way.

Clare sat down and asked if I'd like to have the day room while I'm here. The day room is like a big lounge, with books and games and a TV. Clare said if I go in there, I can have people visit me any time, as many as I like. At the moment, even my family can't all visit at the same time. Two visitors at a time is the rule, and since Mum is here most of the time, that means one other person.

So I've got the day room. It's great! Jodie might be able to visit. I'd really like to see her. And all my family can come together, including Grandma and Grandad. Granny works at the hospital shop, so she could come and see me whenever she wanted, even before I got the day room. I like it when she comes. And she brings me Chocolate Buttons as well. The Chocolate Buttons remind me of when I was about 3, and there was a lady at church who always had some chocolate for me in her bag. She must have been as old as some of the people here. I remember she had a gold tooth; every time she gave me the chocolate, she smiled, and sometimes I was so busy staring at the tooth that I nearly forgot to take the chocolate!

Same tie every day

The last few days since I've had the day room have been better. The only time I have to go back onto the ward bit is

24

when the nurses want to check my temperature, or blood pressure, or give me steroids. And to sleep, obviously; they didn't move my bed into the day room! Every morning, Dr Disney comes to check on me, and he always wears the Disney tie. I don't know if it's normal for doctors to wear the same tie every day, but I really like seeing it. It makes me smile. Oh, and I go back to eat, too, but apart from that I could almost forget I'm in hospital.

Yesterday someone from my English class came to see me. She brought five books our teacher had given her to give me. They're not books I have to read for college, just books I might like. I knew I have the best English teacher in college! I can't wait till this brain tumour stuff is over.

Jodie is going to come soon. I'm waiting for her now, because she said she'd come between her classes. She's doing geography, which will hopefully help her find her way on the huge hospital map. Ha ha.

I'd better go and take my steroids.

Shy

Jodie has just left, *much* later than planned. Soon after she got here, a nurse came to tell me I had a phone call. It was someone from our church youth group, wondering if some of them could come to visit. Now, what I haven't told you is that I'm quite shy and nervous in some ways. OK, lots of ways. When I was 10, my family

25

went on holiday, and I didn't even dare go to the shop nearby on my own! I always asked Sophie to come with me.

So after this phone call, I said to Jodie could she stay. I needed her to give me confidence, I think, just like I sometimes do with Sophie. And she did! She actually skipped school for me. I think that's really brave. I'd never dare skip school, but I'm glad Jodie is braver than me.

Photos of my brain

I've been in hospital for a week now. It seems longer, and it's weird; it's like the world outside hospital doesn't really exist. But I'll see for myself that it exists soon. Dr Disney says I can leave the ward, and leave the hospital! Isn't that great? It feels like ages since I went outside. It's not because I'm better – I wish – but it's so I can go to another hospital and see another doctor. Apparently, the week of taking steroids has got me stable enough to travel.

Mum and Dad came to pick me up. Dad's got a day off work. Dad never takes days off work. As we left the ward, Clare gave me a brown envelope to give to the new doctor I was going to see. The envelope contains those photos of my brain. That's not a normal thing to carry around, is it?

It took about forty minutes to drive to the other hospital, but I didn't mind, I was just glad to be out. When we got to

Nottingham – where the other hospital is – we stopped to get me some food. Steroids make me hungry! Then we went to the hospital. It's massive. Are all hospitals massive? Dad read the map, Mum and I just followed him until we got to the doctor's office. When we got inside, the doctor told me to sit on the black chair in the middle of the room. It was like a dentist's chair, but bigger. I mean, a lot bigger. I had to climb into it! When I was sitting, my feet didn't reach the footrest. I looked at the doctor. He opened the envelope and studied the pictures of my brain. How has 'pictures of my brain' become a normal sentence in just a week? When he'd finished, he cleared his throat and said:

'You know you have two brain tumours? We need to operate. We'll remove one tumour first and, as you know, when we have done so, you will be deaf.'

It was as though the chair started spinning. Fast.

I couldn't focus on the doctor any more. I couldn't focus on anything, except one word.

Deaf

Deaf?! I'm going to be deaf?

What was he talking about? I'm not cut out to be deaf. What about all my music?

I managed to focus back on him, and heard him say, 'It's possible the operation will cause damage to your facial nerve.'

What? Deaf *and* unable to smile? How am I even sitting here? This is not my life.

But even as I thought it, I knew this had become my life. After the appointment, we got in the car to go back to the hospital in Leicester. On the way, we talked a bit about what the doctor had said. I realized that I wouldn't go deaf in both ears after this operation, the doctor had said I would only be deaf on one side. Only. Ha.

I was really hungry (again), so Mum and I kept asking Dad to stop somewhere, but he just kept driving. It was like he couldn't stop. Finally, he stopped somewhere really close to 'my' hospital. We ate – I was really, really hungry – and then went back to the hospital. I knew I was going to be discharged. The new doctor had said I needed to take the steroids for about another month before he would operate. I could do that at home.

So, two things I can do for the next month: a) take steroids b) lie still in bed so the tumours stabilize.

Lie in bed, doing nothing.

For four weeks.

Grandma

I forgot to write that before we went back to the hospital, we went to see my grandparents, to tell them about the operation and me being deaf. Grandma cried. She never cries.

Psalm 73:26

I think this is the worst situation I've ever been in. Worse than being bullied, worse than sitting in A&E, worse than everything put together. Lying here, staring at the ceiling, I remember all the times Mum has said to me, 'Let's pray about it.' It's always the first thing we do. OK, I can still pray.

'God? God?'

Sometimes people say they feel that their prayers are bouncing off a ceiling, which means they don't feel like they are getting through to God. I always used to think, 'I don't know what you mean.' But now I do know.

It's not that I don't believe God is there, and with me, it's just really hard to talk to him at the moment, you know? I've never felt like this before.

I can read my Bible, though, so that's good. It reminds me that God is close.

One verse I read this morning (Psalm 73:26) sort of jumped out at me.

> 'My mind and my body may become weak.
> But God is my strength.
> He is mine forever.'

It jumped out at me because the first bit is basically talking about me. It's like my body is doing weird things and growing tumours. Oh, I forgot to tell you. It's not only tumours in the brain.

Apparently the tumours will just grow on nerves in my body, anywhere they like.

So my body is weak; I could see that when I failed all those tests Dr Disney made me do. But then the verse says, 'God is my strength.' That must mean that even when rubbish stuff is happening, God will help me get through it? I think it does mean that.

Please pray?

Mum came into my bedroom just now, with food. The steroids are making me hungrier and hungrier. I've put on weight, and they are giving me spots.

As I bit into a sandwich, Mum said that she'd been thinking. I thought, 'Oh no, I don't think I'm going to like this!'

She said she'd been thinking we need to ask other people to pray for us.

OK . . .

Then she said she was going to send out emails telling people what was going on with me – exactly what was going on – so they could pray.

I stopped chewing my sandwich. No way was I letting that happen. As if I want people knowing about my life! Also, this brain tumour stuff will soon be over; the doctor said I'll only be in hospital for ten days after the operation. After that I'm going back to college and normal life.

So I said no. But Mum said yes and, in the end, I agreed. It won't be for long, anyway, will it?

Unreal

My operation is two weeks today. Brain surgery. I still can't believe this is happening.

Surprise!

I got a surprise parcel today! It's from my
friends. They've recorded music and messages
for me to listen to. They can't visit me at
the moment, and I don't really want to talk
on the phone – I don't have anything to say – but it's great
to hear their voices. Jodie said, 'I know we won't always be
together, but we will always be close.' I hope she's right.

Photo

Three days to go until surgery. Today, I'm allowed to get up
and go out. Not for long, but the doctor still said I could; I
have to be careful and everything, but they said I could go.
It's to a photo studio, to have a photo of all our family taken,
including grandparents, so that means nine of us. I'm going
to wear my favourite red dress. My face is all bloated and
spotty – steroids' fault again.

There's a reason we are having this photo. And there is a *reason* we
are having this photo. The reason is because it will be nice. The
reason, which we don't really say out loud, is that brain surgery is
serious, and I might die. Even if I don't die, I might wake up with
a wonky face. So this might be the last photo of us all together.

(Later) I'm back. The photo was really weird. We were all
pretending everything was fine, but I had to stand in the
middle in the photo because I'm the one who might die. I
know I'll look spotty.

I don't know when we'll see the photo.

I'm glad to be back in bed. I can't believe how tired that trip out of the house made me.

Tomorrow

Aunty Jane and Granny came to stay today. Tomorrow, Mum and Dad will take me to the hospital and Aunty Jane and Granny will look after my sisters. My operation is the day after tomorrow. I wish I could stay at home with Aunty Jane and Granny.

Hospital

I'm at the hospital now. Operation is tomorrow, and it's my birthday in five days' time. When I was 9, my birthday was the last one Grandpa came to in the family before he died, which means he's not been here for eight years. I'm not glad he died, but I am glad he never had to know that his granddaughter has tumours. I wish none of my family had to know it.

24/7

When I'm in the operation, someone is going to be praying for me every second. My uncle – well, he's not my real uncle, but he's like an uncle – has arranged a timetable and people at church all signed up to pray at different times, even at night-time. It's amazing they would do that for me, isn't it?

Not scared

I'm not scared. Even though I'm being taken to an operating theatre, to spend the next twelve hours having my brain operated on, I know it'll be OK. When the tumour has gone, my headache will be sorted, and after ten days in hospital, I'll be home and back at college.

My surgeon is called Mr Taylor. He's not the one I saw who had the dentist's chair; Dr Dentist Chair passed me on to Mr Taylor. I like Mr Taylor. He has a Scottish accent and is really nice. He tells me about his family; he's got four children, just like my mum and dad have, but the youngest is a boy. Mr Taylor and my dad joke about being surrounded by girls, but I can tell they like it really. Mr Taylor is a neurosurgeon.

I have to go in an anaesthetic room first, to be put to sleep for the operation. I am a bit scared now, but Mum's allowed into the anaesthetic room with me. I'm really glad she's here. I'm lying on the bed in the middle of the room. Well, it's not really a bed, it's more like a narrow bench. I've got a thin blue blanket on me, but it doesn't stop me shivering. Someone has just put a needle, called a cannula, into a vein in the back of my hand, and it will give me medication during the operation. Mr Taylor came in to see me. I didn't expect that! Everyone is wearing blue pyjamas, called scrubs. It's like a uniform. I wish I was back at school in my school uniform. Mr Taylor looks really different! He's got a cap thing on as well. Someone has injected something into my cannula to help me relax. (Because this is such a relaxing situation. Not.) Now someone else is putting a plastic mask over my face and nose, which will put me to sleep. They tell me to take deep breaths, but I don't think they know that the plastic smells really bad. It stinks! I try to move away but they hold the mask there, pinning it to my face. I can't breathe. They tell me to count backwards from ten. I don't think they know I am rubbish at maths! They should have asked me to do the alphabet. The smell is making me feel sick.

'My mind and my body may become weak.
But God is my strength.'
Ten, nine, eight . . .

Smiling

Mum is sitting by my bed. I'm lying down and I've just woken up. My head feels really sore, and there's a big 'nothing' noise in my left ear. I didn't know silence could be so loud. Mum sees I'm awake, and she leans over and holds my hand. I turn my head on the pillow to look at her. Ouch. 'Em; they saved your face.' I can still smile. Did you get that? I can still smile!

I'm fine!

Mum is sitting by my bed again. My head is still sore and wrapped in a massive bandage, but I'm doing OK. I can sit up now. Maybe soon I'll be able to try walking. A nurse came round and asked if I was hungry, which is why I'm eating strawberry yoghurt. Strawberries are my favourite. Mum and I are talking. I still feel tired and sore, but I think I was right; everything will be fine.

ICU

It's a long time since I wrote in my diary. What I write now is what I've been told. I can't remember it, and even when I started remembering things, I couldn't write – not at first, anyway. You'll see what I mean because I've written that bit down now, so there isn't a big gap.

Soon after I ate that strawberry yoghurt, Mum noticed my left foot was really cold (I don't know how she noticed that). Then I became unconscious, which means it was like I was asleep and no one could wake me up. Mum called the doctors to my bed, and they said they needed to do another operation because when they removed the tumour, it left a space, and the space had filled with brain fluid, which was squashing my brainstem. Dad had gone home the day before, thinking everything was fine, and then came back to visit. When he got to the hospital, he came straight to my ward, but before he got there, he bumped into us in the corridor.

I was being pushed on my bed and one doctor was kneeling on my bed, being pushed along too. He was pumping air into me by hand, to keep me alive. So Dad got a shock. In the operation this time, they put a shunt in my head. A shunt is a sort of tube thing that helps get rid of the fluid. But I still didn't wake up, and was taken to intensive care (ICU). ICU is where people go if they are really, really poorly. After two days, Mr Taylor told Mum and Dad that he wanted to operate again, to try to find out why I wasn't waking up. So, on my 17th birthday, the birthday I was supposed to be learning to drive a car, I was back in theatre. After that, I still didn't wake up, and Mr Taylor said I had to go back into ICU. When I was there, a machine kept me alive. It breathed for me because I couldn't breathe for myself, and Mr Taylor even came in to check on me at the weekend, when he doesn't normally work. After about a week in ICU, Mr Taylor asked Mum and Dad for permission to switch off my life-support machine. He said I would never wake up.

Mum and Dad said yes. They didn't want me to die, but they knew that if I did, I would go to heaven, because I'd trusted my life to Jesus; I remember doing that when I was 5, in my bed (I had the top bunk bed, Sophie had the bottom one).

All my family came to say goodbye to me before the machine was switched off. I'm glad I don't remember that.

Then the doctors and nurses and Mum and Dad stood round my bed, ready to switch my life support off. At the last minute, one of the doctors said, 'Stop!' He'd seen that maybe I did have a chance to live, after all, so the machine was not switched off. But I could do nothing. I couldn't move. I couldn't even breathe for myself. Oh yes, I could do one thing: I could hear from my right ear. I didn't know you could still hear when you're unconscious, but you can. So my dad sat by my bed for hours, saying, 'Breathe. Breathe. Breathe . . .' I would only breathe if someone told me to, so Dad told me to. Eventually, when I'd learned to breathe without being told, the life-support machine was taken away. I became conscious again.

Squiggles

After I woke up, I was still in ICU, because I was still really poorly and couldn't move. I couldn't even talk! Can you imagine not being able to talk? It's so frustrating. If I wanted to tell people something, they had to get a piece of paper, hold a pencil in my hand, and move the paper for me to write on. Well, when I say 'write' I mean make squiggles for letter shapes, really. I'm too weak to move my arm.

I can't eat and am being fed through a tube the nurses stuck up my nose. It hurts my nose.

Ragdoll

Today, I found the strength to pull the tube out of my nose. My arm flopped about and the tube lay on my blankets, spurting out stuff that looked like sick. So, I've been having sick pumped into me. Great. Actually, I still am because a nurse has just put another tube in. I'm not in ICU now, I'm on a ward. Not the same one as before my operation; there wasn't a bed for me on the other ward, because I'd been in ICU for so long. This ward is called a medical ward. I should really be on the surgical ward, because I've had surgery; no one else on this ward seems to have had surgery. A lot of them wander off, and the nurses keep bringing them back. One lady thinks I'm her granddaughter. I don't know why, she's definitely not my grandma! Or my granny. She really scares me. She comes right up close to my bed, and I can't move. She sometimes grabs my hand and pulls. I'm glad I have cot sides on my bed, so she can't pull me out. I wouldn't be able to stop her. I'm just like a ragdoll lying here.

Skinny

Useless. I can't move at all. The nurses have to come and roll me into a different position every few hours, so I don't get bed sores. Bed sores are things you get if you don't move and pressure is on one part of your body for too long. So if my hip was on the bed for ages, and I wasn't moved, I'd get a bedsore on my hip. Especially if you're skinny, which I am! I've lost all the weight from the steroids. The sickfood-tube obviously didn't help, and I'm not hungry anyway. Sometimes the nurses forget to move me, and that makes Mum really cross. Sometimes she goes away at night, comes back in the morning, and I haven't moved at all! I think the nurses are just trying to stop other patients escaping, and it's not as though I can escape, is it? I wonder if I'll ever be able to move again.

Perfume

I can still smell, even though
I can't move. I smell Mum's
perfume every day when she comes. And she always wears a
nice dress, too. She told me it's hot weather outside.

Can't move

It'll soon be July. I still can't move.

Pathetic

The nurses are trying to get me to eat, but I'm still not
hungry. Mum is trying, too. Today, she came to my bed with
a bowl of Weetabix in her hand. It was a white bowl, and she
wanted me to eat the Weetabix. I didn't want to, but I wanted
to please her, so I tried. I couldn't lift the spoon to my mouth –
still too weak – so Mum fed me, just like she did when I was
a baby. I really, really tried to eat, but in the end I was too full
and had to say I'd had enough. When I looked in the bowl,
most of the Weetabix was still there. I'd been eating for ages,
but I'd hardly eaten anything. How pathetic. Don't you think
it's pathetic? I can't even eat a Weetabix. But Mum said, 'Well
done.' She was glad I'd tried, and she thought I'd done well. I
still felt pathetic, but I felt a bit better about it too.

Well done?

Well done.

Kirsty

My sister Kirsty came to visit today. It's a school day! I couldn't believe she'd been allowed a day off school. We are *never* allowed a day off school unless we are really poorly. Kirsty has been poorly but she's OK now. I think she should have been at school, but I was happy to see her (as well as being a bit cross). So Kirsty was here when the physiotherapists came. They've been coming the last few days to try to get me moving. First they moved the backrest on my bed so I was sitting up. It was awful! I was sick. I don't know why brain surgery and lying flat for weeks makes you sick when you sit up, but it does. But they've tried it a few more times since, and now I can sit without being sick. A few days ago they moved my legs so I was sitting on the edge of the bed with my feet on the floor. One of the physios knelt on the bed behind me, to stop me falling over. Yep, I'm still so weak I can't even hold myself in a sitting position. I sat there for a minute, then I asked them to let me lie down again, so they lowered me back onto the bad. I was so tired, just from sitting. It's really weird. I still feel like the person who runs cross-country, but my body doesn't seem to get it.

Australia

Every day the nurse asks me where I am.
I know I'm in Australia, but every time
I tell her that, she says, 'It would be nice
if you were, but no you're not, you're in
England.' Now I've learned that she wants me to say 'England'
but in my head I always add, 'I know I'm in Australia really.'

Today I realized I am in England, after all. I've been
hallucinating for the last five days when I said 'Australia' each
time. I think it's because I have a high temperature, and my
brain got mangled in surgery.

I really did go to Australia when I was 3, and Mum told me I
hallucinated there as well. It was when I was poorly and had
a high temperature, and I kept telling her there were koalas
in my bedroom. I don't know how long it took me to realize
there weren't any really. But koalas are cute. I'd rather have a
koala in my bedroom than be in hospital right now!

Sitting

Now the physios want me to sit in the chair by my bed. They
brought a big frame with some material on it and said I would
go in the material, a bit like a hammock, and get swung from
my bed to my chair. It's called a hoist and its really scary
going in it. I've done it a few times now, and then I have to
sit in the chair for hours. I just beg anyone who will listen to
let me get back into bed. Seriously, it's exhausting sitting in

the chair. And the seat material is slippery, so I keep slipping down but have no strength to pull myself up again. Last time I went in the hoist, Mum was there, and it's a good thing she was because when they'd got me in the air and were moving me across to the chair, I started falling out of the hoist. I'm too weak to help myself, and Mum caught me and stopped me slipping out of the gap in the material. I'm so skinny, I slip through it! And that's the end of the hoist for me. Good.

Eye

No one told me that brain surgery would make my eye dry! It won't make tears by itself, now, and I have to put eyedrops in all the time because my eye is really sore. Correction; someone else has to put eyedrops in for me. I can't even do that for myself.

Standing

Today when the physios came, they said they wanted to get me standing. Now, when they sit me on the edge of the bed, I can support myself. I still can't move my legs over, but I can sit. The physio was carrying what looked like a thing that old people use to walk with; I've seen them when I go to play the piano at an old people's home.

43

I go once a month and play while the people who live there sing. At Christmas it's Christmas songs, otherwise it's hymns. They like old ones best; I think they remember them from when they were young, and after we've sung the songs, I close the lid of the piano and then go and chat with people. Mostly they are sitting in chairs, but I can kneel on the floor beside them and talk. Sometimes they remember me, sometimes they don't. Sometimes one of the people who looks after them will come to take them somewhere, and I watch them shuffle away, pushing a Zimmer frame to help them walk. A frame exactly like the one the physiotherapist is holding. Why won't my body understand that I can walk?

And that I'm not old.

I grabbed hold of the Zimmer, and one physio held it steady while two more went each side of me. They counted 'one, two, three' and then lifted me. I was standing up. I felt sick and dizzy and just wanted to be back in bed.

Zimmer frame

I'm getting a bit stronger every day. I'm still really skinny but I'm just not hungry. Now when the physios bring the Zimmer, I can push with my arms and sit up without help. I can nearly stand by myself. Well, with the help of the Zimmer, but I'm not mentioning that. Still can't believe I'm using a Zimmer!

I can walk a few steps with it, but the physios always take it away when they go. They say it's not safe for me to try on my own. I really wish I could walk far enough to get to the toilet without having to call for a nurse to help.

Cards

I get a card every morning!
Aunty Jane – I bet she never
thought she'd be looking after my sisters for this long – sends me a card every day. Aunty Jane taught me to read and write before I even went to school. Sometimes the card tells me how things are at home. Other times it reminds me that lots of people are praying for me, and that God loves me. It's nice to be reminded. I never stopped believing God loves me. Why would God stop loving me, just because I'm in hospital?

Forgetting

I can remember Aunty Jane taught me to read, but I forget what happened five minutes ago. Mr Taylor said my short-term memory was affected by the brain surgery, but my long-term memory is OK. So I can remember I am learning about memory in psychology class at college. I like psychology. We never learned that brain surgery can ruin short-term memory, though. Earlier today, Mum was visiting me and she needed to go to the toilet. When she got back, I said, 'Hello, Mum, I've not seen you for ages.' But she has been here every day I've been in hospital! And that's a *lot* of days.

I can still remember how to read, but that's another thing that's weird. All my life, people have said that I devour books. That means I read them really quickly and spend a lot of time reading. But now, I just can't concentrate on reading, and I forget what I've read anyway, so have to read pages again and again. Mum had an idea: she saw a magazine in the hospital shop that has short stories in, so she brought me that to try. I hope it works. I'm really fed up just lying here in hospital. I've been here for weeks now.

Chocolate or teddy bear?

Today, the physios brought a wheelchair. I never would have thought I'd be glad to go in a wheelchair, but it means I can go out of the ward for a bit! I must be getting stronger if they'll let me do that. It took a while to get into the chair. My feet kept slipping off the footrests because my legs aren't strong enough to stop them, but at last Mum could push me off the ward and into the main hospital. I've been really worried because I saw the date on some doctors' notes, and so I know Jodie's birthday is coming up, and I haven't got her a present. Mum said it doesn't matter and that Jodie would understand, but it really matters to me. Jodie and I never miss each other's birthdays. So today Mum pushed me to the hospital shop to choose a present for Jodie. There wasn't much to choose from; it was either chocolates or a teddy bear. I chose teddy bear, and I chose a card as well. Just so you know, a teddy bear like that is not what I would normally choose for a 17th birthday present! That tired me out and so we went back to the ward. When I was back in bed, I tried to write the card for Jodie. I can't even hold a pen! Well, not properly. I can write better than when

46

people had to move the paper for me, but still not even as well as I could when Aunty Jane first taught me, when I was 3! I managed to write 'Happy Birthday Jodie love from Emily' but it just looked like scribbly writing. My writing is usually messy. Last time I had an essay marked at college, my teacher wrote 'I can't read this' on it. If even she couldn't read it, my writing must be bad! But it's not shaky-scribbly messy. Jodie's card looks like a 2-year-old wrote it.

I felt really sad when I looked at that writing.

Spinning

It's Mum's birthday the day after Jodie's, and Dad took me to the same shop to choose a card for her. Sometimes Dad spins me in my wheelchair in the hospital corridors. Mum never does that! Maybe that's because Mum went in a wheelchair for a while when she hurt her knee, so she knows what it's like. But I like it when Dad spins me (even though I'm a bit scared, too) because I know he's trying to make things a bit better for me.

We chose a card for Mum. My writing in it is still rubbish. I hate it.

Mirror

To get to the shop, we had to go down in a lift. The lift is big enough for a wheelchair, or even two or three, but the lift doesn't have walls. It has mirrors. Do lifts always have mirrors? I've never noticed before. Maybe it's just hospital lifts. So, there I was, sitting in a wheelchair, unable to move, but it wasn't the chair that trapped me. It was the mirror. I was facing it and I couldn't move. I had to either shut my eyes or look in the mirror. I looked in the mirror, but it wasn't me looking back. Half my hair was shaved off! And the rest looked like straw. That's not my hair. I look as rubbish as I feel. I'm glad the hospital is too far away from home for many people to visit me. My family come, and my grandparents, but that's it, thank goodness.

Games

Mum, Dad and I play 'Chase the Ace' a lot. Have you ever played it? It's a card game, and we play it for hours, taking it in turns to put a card on the table by my bed. All the beds in hospital have their own table, but there's not much space to play cards. We have to make sure we don't knock my water jug over, or push the grey bowl off the table. The grey bowl is there in case I'm sick. It's made of cardboard, I think, and it smells really bad. Even if I don't feel sick, one whiff of that bowl is enough to make me feel queasy!

Tennis

Wimbledon is on at the moment.
I love tennis; Sophie and I play
tennis together. When we went on holiday to France, Sophie and I spent lots of time at the campsite tennis courts. At home, the courts are concrete, but in France they were red. Dad said it's

called clay-court. In hospital, Mum and I watch Wimbledon. I have a tiny little TV screen I can watch from my bed, so Mum lies down next to me and we watch it together. Normally we go to Grandma and Grandad's house to watch Wimbledon.

The physios leave my Zimmer by my bed now, so I can practise standing. I still can't walk to the toilet by myself, but I think the Zimmer-at-the-end-of-the-bed must mean I'm getting a bit better. I hope it does.

Park

It's been a while since I first got the wheelchair. I can sit in it better now, though my feet still slip. The physios have said I can go outside! The real outside, not just to a different part of the hospital. The last time I was outside was when I came into hospital. I could walk, then, you know. So today my whole family is coming over and they are going to take me out. My sisters told me they've found a park near the hospital that has a smooth path, and it will be a good place to take me. I'm a bit scared about going out of the hospital. Part of me really wants to go, but part of me only wants to want to go, if you see what I mean; that's the part that wants to stay. What if something happens and there are no doctors or nurses to look after me?

Jokes

I survived going out, but I'm glad to be back. When we got out of the hospital, my dad pushed me over the road to the

49

park, then my sisters all wanted a turn at pushing. Sophie and Kirsty were fine, but Pollyanna is so small she couldn't see where she was going! So she just pushed, and I held onto the red wheelchair handles as tightly as I could.

Pollyanna is eight years younger than me. Or seven, depending on who has had a birthday. Really she is seven-and-a-half-minus-one-day years younger. When I had only been in hospital a few weeks and still could not sit up, Pollyanna would bring her joke book to read me jokes. She *loves* jokes!

Here's one of them:

> Knock Knock
> Who's there?
> Owl
> Owl who?
> Owl you know unless you open the door?

Ha ha, it is quite funny!

Today the doctor said I can go back to the hospital near home. But I'm not better. I still can't walk. I thought I would be better when I leave hospital?

Ambulance

I'm back at the other hospital now, the one with Dr Disney. I've not seen him yet, but Nurse Clare is here, and she remembers me! I wonder if Dr Disney

will remember me, too. I'm on the same ward as last time, but this time, I'm in the bed furthest away from the nurses' desk, which means they think I'm doing OK. It doesn't feel like I'm doing OK; all I can do is lie here. I came in an ambulance and I asked if they'd put the flashing blue light on, but they said no, I wasn't an emergency. I had to be strapped onto a bed and lie in the back of the ambulance, covered in a red blanket. I was glad of the blanket. I know it's nearly July, but I felt cold. Mum came in the ambulance with me, and I think I must have slept, because the journey didn't take long. If we go on a long journey, Mum always tells my sisters to sleep and the journey will be over quicker. She doesn't say that to me, because she knows I'll just read my book.

Sad

It's really quiet at this end of the ward. There are six beds in my bay (room) but often there's only two or three patients in here. Today there was just me and one other lady; my bed is in one corner and hers is the other end of the bay. She's a bit like me because walking is hard for her, but she's a bit better than me because she can actually walk around her bed. I saw her get out of bed and then start walking. Then I saw her fall over! Literally flat on the floor. I really wished I could go over and help, but I couldn't because of my stupid legs; why won't they work? So I pressed the button by my bed that calls the nurse, and Clare came. Everything was fine, the lady was OK, but I felt really sad that I couldn't help.

Exciting!

I've been doing the strengthening
exercises on my legs that the physios
at the other hospital told me to do,
and I'm getting stronger and stronger. Guess what happened
today? I shuffled to the toilet! *I can now shuffle to the toilet by
myself with my Zimmer! I do not have to call for a nurse to take
me. Yes!*

Gym

Now I can stand and shuffle, the new physio said it's time for
me to try the gym. She took me down there in my wheelchair
today, stopped my chair by two bars – called parallel bars –
and said I could hold onto them and walk in-between them.
I don't think so. Maybe the old me could, the real me. But
the me-I-am-at-the-moment cannot walk. And the me-I-
am-at-the-moment has feet which still slip off the wheelchair
footrests, just to remind me how weak I am. But the physio
seemed to think I could do it, so I grabbed the bars and
hauled myself out of the chair. I stood there with shaking legs.
Eventually I took one step. Then another. And another. It was
really slow, but I was walking. Kind of. About halfway down,
my legs gave way and another physio pushed my wheelchair
behind me and caught me. The bars aren't even as long as half
a small classroom at college.

Banana milkshake

Now I'm in a hospital close to home, my sisters
can come to visit me every evening after school.
But I have three sisters, and only two visitors
are allowed. I've not got the day room this time.
There's no point, I can't get to it! And anyway, I
don't really want other visitors. So Nurse Clare
makes one of my sisters wait outside the ward
while two visit, then swap, but now, Clare told
me that if I want, my family can take me out in
my wheelchair to the café or somewhere, as long as I am back
by 9 p.m. That's really good because I feel bad that my sisters
have to sit outside.

About a week ago, Mum and Dad were visiting me and I
suddenly said, 'I would really like a McDonald's banana
milkshake.' Mum and Dad were surprised. Even I was
surprised! I haven't been interested in food or drink since
before my operation. Milkshakes are something I do with
Sophie, ever since we were allowed into town by ourselves. I
have banana milkshake, she has strawberry.

The day after I said I'd like a milkshake, when Dad visited,
he brought me one. And every single day since, either he or
Grandad bring me one. They never forget. It's funny thinking
of my grandad going into McDonald's. I bet this is the first
time he's ever been in there!

McDonald's

Dad didn't bring a milkshake today, because he said they were all going to take me out and I could buy one myself. So we went to McDonald's. Me in my wheelchair. I know I look silly, I saw myself again in the lift mirror. People stare at me but I try to ignore them, like I ignored the bullies at school. I don't like it, though, and I'm embarrassed to go out, but it was good at McDonald's, even though I didn't dare buy my own milkshake. It's the first time I've ever been with my family, because we never go to McDonald's all together. It's just not something we do, but things are different now.

I was glad to get back to the hospital. I feel safe here.

Mum's birthday

Mum's birthday is tomorrow, and Clare said I can go home for it! I have to come back to the hospital at night, but I can go home.

I don't know if my wheelchair will fit through the front door of my house.

I don't know how I'll get up the steps.

An hour

I feel rubbish. I'm back in my hospital bed and the lights are out; I should be asleep but I can't stop thinking about today. I ruined Mum's birthday. I managed to get into the car, and my wheelchair did fit through the front door of the house, but as soon as I sat down in the lounge, I wanted to get back to the hospital. My family had planned a really nice day and I didn't even want to be there. I tried not to let it show. I mean, how stupid not to even be able to stay at home, and wanting to go back to hospital, of all places? I really tried not to let it show, but Mum guessed. I said I was fine but, after only an hour – before Mum had even opened any cards or presents – they took me back to the hospital. I ruined the day. Stupid hospital. Stupid me.

Secret

I'm getting a bit stronger. Every day, the physios take me down to the gym, and I can walk between the parallel bars now. Someone called an occupational therapist (OT) came to see me when I was on the ward. She said she wants to see what I can do, and will come back tomorrow, because the doctors and people say I can go home soon. For good. That is really scary, but don't tell anyone I said so, OK? I know I need to be brave.

Mickey Mouse

It was fun with the OT! We went to a kitchen in the hospital and made tea and cakes. It reminded me how weak and uncoordinated I am, though. I could hardly pick up the kettle, and I had to hold on to the counter with one hand all the time to stop me falling over, but I managed to make a cup of tea, and I managed to put Mickey Mouse decorations on each of the little pink cakes. I had to put them on with my left hand because that's the one that has been really damaged, and I need to try using it more. Who'd have thought brain surgery would damage my hand? I suppose it's good it's not my right hand, because I'm right-handed. That one is weak, too, but not as weak. I don't know how I will manage to play my music when my fingers don't really want to do things. OT was more fun than physio; physio is really hard work.

Funny!

Jodie came to visit today when it was time for physio, so she pushed me down to the gym in my wheelchair. Well, it wasn't mine, it was one of the hospital ones, and everyone finds them hard to push. Jodie couldn't push it straight! We lurched all the way down the long corridor to the gym. It was really funny.

TV

I've got to go home for a night, then a weekend, then – in the end – for good. Big surprise as well: we are getting a TV! It's to help try to get my memory working. Some programmes are on every day, and you follow the storyline. I've never seen them but I know people talk about them.

Whoops!

I was at home yesterday and overnight, and it was a bit better this time. My family took me to the park in my wheelchair, and Dad was pushing me across a field when the wheel got stuck and the chair tipped forward and I flew out. I just lay there on the grass. I'm too weak to even get myself up. When everyone realized I was OK, Dad started laughing. I did, too. It must have looked a bit funny, me flying out of my chair and landing splat! Mum didn't think it was funny, though, and she told Dad he should have been more careful.

Alive

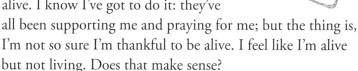

Church have organized a special service called a Thanksgiving Service, to say thank you to God that I'm alive. I know I've got to do it: they've all been supporting me and praying for me; but the thing is, I'm not so sure I'm thankful to be alive. I feel like I'm alive but not living. Does that make sense?

Back to normal

When I left the hospital for the last time, I felt sad, which is weird because I should be happy. Being home is OK. Mum's cooking is better than hospital food. I still have to go back to hospital for physio, but now I'm called an outpatient, which means I don't stay at the hospital. I can walk a little bit with crutches now, and I'm learning to sometimes go without them, even though I still have to use my wheelchair if I go far. I feel like I might be getting back to normal. I still have the loud silence in one ear, which is really hard, but apart from that I'm OK and getting stronger all the time. I never want to see another hospital again. Life needs to go back to normal, even though I'm still waiting for my shaved hair to grow back. I need to go back to college, but *everyone* except me thinks that is a bad idea. They want me to wait, or go back into Year 12. But I'm not in Year 12, I'm in Year 13. I know I missed a term of Year 12, and I know I spent the summer in hospital, but I can do it. I do remember I am good at lessons.

It was my English teacher who stuck up for me. Everyone else said I should not go back into Year 13, but she said if that's what I wanted to do, that's what I should do. I'm going to have a taxi to and from college because I can't walk that far any more, but apart from that, things are going back to normal.

I can't wait.

Sign language

I am not good at lessons.

I'd forgotten I can't remember things now. So in psychology, where I have to remember names and dates, it's impossible. In English, I can't remember what I've just read in the book. How am I supposed to write essays? I've stopped music and French: it's hard enough doing two A levels. So things *aren't* back to normal. It's so weird how I can remember I used to be able to remember things. Now I look at a page of psychology dates and I'm asking my brain why it won't remember. I get really mad with my brain; it's so frustrating. I'm not playing hockey any more, either. My eye is sore, too. Remember I told you brain surgery left my eye dry? I have learned to put the drops in it myself now, but it's still really sore. Oh, and another thing. Mum says we have to learn sign language, because one day, when I have the other surgery, I'll be deaf. But I don't think that will happen to me, I really don't. I'm not a deaf person. She's worrying about nothing. A little part of me worries she's right, but I ignore that part. There's no point in learning sign language, but Mum says we have to, so every Thursday, Mum, Dad, my sisters and I will spend three hours learning to speak sign language. *Three hours*. What a nightmare.

Reminder

I don't like Thursdays. I hate learning sign language. I'm rubbish at it, and it reminds me that one day I might be deaf. Who needs that? Pollyanna is really good at sign language. She's 9.

No life

It was the Thanksgiving Service at church today, and I sat there in my wheelchair, half my hair still shaved, hardly able to sit up straight. I was surrounded by people thanking God for me and my life, I even chose songs to sing at the service, but I wasn't thanking God for me and my life. I think, if I can't go back to my old life – Before Tumours Life – I'd be better not to have a life. And that's the truth.

Decision

I still have to go to see doctors to be checked and, last time, they told me I should see a geneticist. A geneticist is a doctor who works out why I've got NF2. So that's where I am now, with Mum and Dad. It's really strange here, not like a normal hospital. It's got comfy chairs, and the geneticist has just offered us a drink. Dr Disney and co. have never offered me a drink! I wish the geneticist hadn't. I just want to find out why I'm here, not sit around having a cosy chat. The geneticist said that NF2 is hereditary. That means two things.

1. Maybe Mum or Dad have got NF2 and passed it on to me. And maybe they've passed it on to my sisters as well, so all my family need to be tested to see if they have NF2 in their bodies.
2. If I have children of my own, I will have a 50 per cent chance of passing on NF2 to my child. That's like flipping a coin and saying 'heads the child has NF2 and tails they don't.'

Number 2: Sitting here, drinking tea, in a lounge that's not a lounge, I, Emily, aged 17, decide that I will never have children. Ever. It isn't a hard decision. I have always wanted children, but I can't risk knowingly giving them NF2. It's not fair on them. They'd hate me for it. I'd hate me for it.

Number 1: If any of my sisters has got NF2, I will feel as if it's my fault. I don't know why I'll feel that, but I know I will.

I bet Pollyanna has got it. She's the most like me – or the old me – with being sporty and academic.

Psalm 139

I was reading in my Bible the other day, and I read in Psalm 139 where it says God made us and formed us in our mother's body. I never really used to notice that verse, but now I'm thinking, God made me with tumours? I don't like Psalm 139 now. I love God and I know he loves me, but I can't think about him making me with tumours. It's too hard.

No more NF2

At half-term in October we are going on holiday! To Menorca. It's a special holiday because finally I can walk better, and we can put hospitals behind us. Goodbye to all of them, and good riddance.

Menorca

Menorca was great! The sun shone every day, and we swam in the sea. It was a buffet breakfast in the hotel; eat whatever you wanted. I ate six eggs for breakfast every day!

Ice skating

I've finished my exams now. I know I won't have done well, but I still hope I do. Jodie and I have always said that when we finish our A level exams, we would go ice skating to celebrate. So that's what we did. And that's why we are sitting in A&E. Green chairs this time, not blue. It's the ice skating boots that were blue, and I fell over on the ice and bashed my head. So embarrassing! I tried to just quickly get up, but I kept slipping around. Jodie looked really scared, and because of all my brain surgeries and stuff, the people at the ice rink sent me to hospital. Maybe it wasn't very sensible for me to go ice skating. I was fine at the hospital until I phoned Mum; as soon as I heard her voice, I started to cry. However hard I try to ignore NF2, it ruins everything. Mum came to the hospital to get Jodie and me. It's the same hospital where I had all my brain operations. The doctors said I'm OK, and we drove home. I don't think I'll ever go ice skating again.

Austria

Last week I was in Austria! The band I played in at school invited me to go with them, and we toured around, making music. I played my flute. Making music in beautiful mountains is amazing. I made sure I sat so that the ear I can hear from was towards the rest of the band, and when we were playing, I could almost ignore the 'nothing' noise in my left ear.

As well as playing concerts, we looked around little towns, ate cheese for breakfast, and swam in lakes in the mountains. The water was freezing!

God is there

I am just back from church camp. I was a leader – well, a helper – and lots of teenagers came. Camp is a bit like beach mission, and every night before bed, there is a meeting for everyone in a big tent. One night, the subject for the meeting was 'suffering', and I was asked to talk about that. I was really nervous about standing up in front of everyone! I didn't really know what to say, so I said bad things do happen, but that doesn't mean God's not there. I think that sums it up, really.

Rubbish

Got my A level results. They're rubbish.

Barbie dolls

Everyone is going to university. My dad drove Jodie to hers, and I went too. How is it possible to be 100 per cent happy for Jo while at the same time thinking, 'we were supposed to do this together'? How am I feeling two things at the same time? I hope Jodie enjoys uni. I felt sad when I said goodbye to her.

The day before she left, I went to her house, but we didn't play with Barbie dolls! When we were little, I was soooo jealous of her Barbie doll collection. My mum wouldn't let me have Barbies, so I used to go round to Jodie's and play with hers. She had loads of them, and we played with them for hours. Today we just sat and chatted; it was really nice. Jodie said she's going to see if she can learn sign language at uni. She gave me a little book about Eeyore from *Winnie-the-Pooh*, too.

1998

University

My local university accepted me on their English course! I'm so shocked. It's not Durham, which is where I always wanted to go, but at least it means I can go to university. Uni is OK, and the best thing is that my brain is finally starting to work again, and I'm getting good grades. I am beginning to get a headache, but I think that's just because I'm concentrating hard. My balance is worse, too, but that'll be because I'm tired. I can walk to uni. It takes about half an hour, maybe more, but no need for a taxi any more.

Christian Union

I've started going to the Christian Union at university. It's a bit like a church but in the middle of the week, not on Sundays, and it's mostly

students who go. It's great to be with other people who are following Jesus. I like CU, even though the building where it is means I am right next to the hospital. I don't look at the hospital!

Pretending

I don't think my headache is because of concentrating. I think I know, really, but I pretend I don't. The other tumour must have grown. The one on the right of my brain. The one which will make me completely deaf.

Road drill

Mr Taylor sent me for a scan. One of the ones where I go in a tunnel, and be a gingerbread man in an oven, but Mum didn't hold my foot this time. The people at the hospital say I can listen to music in the scanner, but I don't, because it's really noisy in there, like a road drill. When the road drill pauses, I can hear the music, but then the road drill starts again, and it's really annoying.

The scan showed that I need an operation on the other side of my head from last time. I'm going to be deaf. How can my hearing just be taken away?

Maybe Mum was right about keeping this diary. Who else can I tell stuff to? Real stuff?

Park

I can't stop thinking about not being able to hear. One of the worst things is that I won't be able to hear children. Yesterday I took my little cousin JJ to the park. We talked all the way there and back, but all the time I was thinking, 'Soon I won't be able to hear him.'

The other day, the thought popped into my head that after the operation, the first voice I'll hear will be Jesus, when I get to heaven. That's nice, isn't it? I'm still sad I won't hear children, though.

Drop out

I went with Dad to a meeting at uni, where I had to tell them I was dropping out because I needed brain surgery. I managed not to cry, but my voice wobbled. They were really nice and said I can go back when I'm ready, and that it was a good change to have someone drop out for a real reason. I don't really know what they meant. Why would someone drop out if they didn't have to?

Cross stitch

People at church want to learn sign language. I feel awkward about that. I feel awkward about everything at the moment. But I hate learning sign language, so I feel bad that they want to put themselves through that because of me. And Lizzie is leaving soon. We're really good friends but she was only here while she was at uni. She's finished her degree now, so is going back home. That's miles away. Lizzie made me a cross stitch of that verse I read before my first operation: 'My mind and my body may become weak. But God is my strength. He is mine forever.' She's really good at sewing, not like me. I sewed

a tablecloth once, for Grandma and Grandad, and it took me ages and made me feel grumpy! Lizzie and I always knew she'd be leaving, and we said we'd still talk on the phone, but we didn't know I won't be able to hear when we said that, did we?

Music

Aunty Jane, JJ and TJ have come to stay. It's great to see my little cousins. Practised TJ's song today, to sing at our great-aunt and uncle's Golden Wedding. I'm playing my flute while TJ sings, and he's really nervous, but he's really good! His voice is so sweet. He's only 7, and singing at a dinner is a big thing for him. I'm nervous too, but helping TJ makes it better for me.

I just hope I don't get the giggles on the night! I want it to be nice because it might be the last time I do something like this. That's really weird; I've done family music things like this my whole life.

I babysat TJ tonight, and read him bedtime stories. Will I read children stories when I'm deaf? Will I be able to? I don't know.

Don't know

TJ was brilliant at the dinner last night. He sang 'Where Is Love?' from *Oliver!,* and everyone gave him a massive round of applause.

Today I asked Mum why she thinks I have to go to see Dr Dentist Chair on Wednesday. She didn't know. I hope it doesn't mean things are going even quicker than I expected, and my operation is really soon. Mum and I got pretty upset about it. I don't like making her upset.

Crying

Today I told JJ and TJ that when I have my next operation, it will mean I can't hear them any more. I don't think TJ really knew what I was talking about. Ha, neither do I! JJ was a bit more upset, and he asked his mum if we could all play a game called 'Spit it Out' because soon I won't be able to play it.

'Spit it Out' is one of my favourite games; you have to look at a word on a card and then describe it so your team can guess what the word is. I think JJ means I won't be able to play because I won't be able to hear people's descriptions, or guesses.

I wonder if it's possible to lipread 'Spit it Out'? I wonder if it's really possible to lipread anything? How will I ever read words on people's lips as they speak?

I wanted to tell the boys myself, and I'm glad I did, but it was really hard to tell them about not being able to hear them soon, and it made me cry.

We watched one of those programmes where they show funny things that have happened on TV. One clip showed a news programme where the sound wasn't working, so you could see the person reading the news, but couldn't hear what they were saying. Not so long ago, I might have found it funny, but now when I watched it, I just felt gutted. I'm going to be without sound for the rest of my life.

Bye

Aunty Jane, JJ and TJ went home today. JJ said, 'Bye, good luck in your operation.'

Something on my brain

Saw Dr Dentist Chair. Yes, he still has the chair! I thought he was going to tell me I need the operation now, but he started talking about auditory brainstem implants (ABI). They are things that get put onto your brain. Wondered why he was going on about them and it turned out he's probably going to give me one! If it works, it might give me a bit of sound after I'm deaf, which might help with lipreading. I know I love reading books, but how am I supposed to read words on lips?

I don't know if I want the ABI or not. There's a 20 per cent chance it won't work at all, and if it does work, what if I don't like it? I could switch it off, but then I'd feel guilty about a waste of money. ABIs are *really* expensive.

Dr Dentist Chair said the implant would not affect the chance of saving my facial nerve from being damaged in surgery. If it would have done, I would definitely not have the implant, but now I'm thinking that I might. Dr Dentist Chair said to go into the operation thinking the implant won't work. It's hard to do that.

Dog

We got a dog today! Mum and I went to choose him. He's soooo cute. He's black, with a bit of brown, and his chest is white, and his tail wags *all* the time. That means he's happy. I'm happy we've got him – he won't mind when I can't hear, and I won't need to try to read his lips. He's called Jasper, and he can be my friend.

Why?

Tim, a friend from church, brought round some information about NF2 today, which he'd found on the internet. Some of it was about a 5-year-old who had to have both tumours operated on. He must have been so scared. Why does NF2 happen? I hate it.

Mail

I got letters in the post! *Four!* It's really nice when people write to me and remind me they are thinking of me and tell me about their lives.

Bad mood

Sophie's boyfriend came to stay for the weekend. I wasn't sure about him for her, to be honest, but now I've met him, he seems fine. I've felt in a bad mood for ages now. Maybe it's because of the operation, I don't know.

Reading

Can't be bothered to write much tonight; I'm in the middle of a good book!

Went to a dedication (like a christening) today. It reminded me that I won't ever have children, because of the 50 per cent chance of giving them NF2.

I'm going to read now.

Angry

Church picnic today. It was great, and
we had egg sandwiches. My favourite!
Jasper came to the picnic and he was
very well-behaved, but he kept chasing
the ball when we played rounders.
I've just been playing the piano before
coming to bed. I'll miss the piano so much. Soon I won't
be able to hear. I played a song, written by Noel & Tricia
Richards, called 'By Your Side' ('Your' is God). One of
the lines in the song talks about giving God everything.
Everything means *everything*, doesn't it? So that includes my
tumours and deafness and stuff. I don't think God would
want them.

I'm really angry about the tumour and the operation. Not
angry at God but, like, 'What's going on?' anger. I have so
much more to offer and do when I can hear.

Spying

Went to the Deaf centre today where they showed me
equipment that I can use when I'm deaf. There's this thing
called a minicom, which I can use instead of a phone.
Someone listens into the conversation and types everything
the person I'm calling says, and I can read it on a screen. I
don't think I'll use it more than I have to. It's really weird
to think someone else is listening to my phone call, like
I'm being spied on!

Jasper

Jasper went to train to be a hearing dog, so he could tell me when there is a noise I need to know about, like a doorbell. He'd be able to come into places where it says 'Assistance Dogs Only', and I wouldn't have to leave him outside. But Jasper failed the exam. So now I have to choose: either I have a new dog and get rid of Jasper because Jasper would stop the new dog working, or I keep Jasper and don't have a hearing dog. Guess which I chose? Hint: Jasper is not going anywhere.

Waiting

It's hard just waiting for this operation. I don't really have anything to do, since I stopped uni.

Granny

Aunty Jane phoned and told me that she and JJ and TJ are learning sign language! It's amazing that they'd do that for me.

Granny came round today and met Jasper. She likes him – phew!

Blind?

I've been wishing I was going to be blind, not deaf, because of music. But what about reading? I have to be able to read! But I have to have music as well.

Fish

I got some fish today! Twelve, in a massive tank. I have named them after Jacob's twelve sons in the Bible; don't ask me which is which, though!

Sophie was talking about the band she is in starting up again on Saturday. I hope they have some concerts before my operation so I can hear them.

I need to tidy my bedroom. It's a bit of a mess: clothes and books everywhere; I can hardly see the floor.

Movie

I went out for dinner with Lizzie, then we went to the cinema. I stayed over at her house and we talked really late. When we were watching the movie, I kept thinking about how I won't be able to go to the cinema and watch movies after the op. Everything I do, I seem to be thinking, 'Will I be able to do this after the operation?' The movie was good. Jasper started normal dog training today; hopefully he will be better than he was at hearing dog training.

Subtitles

Took Jasper for a walk, and he did what we did in dog training *reasonably* well. Went to Grandma and Grandad's for dinner, and while we were there, we tried out watching their

TV with the subtitles turned on. It's better than I thought it would be; it does write out most of what is being said. It's hard to read the words and look at the picture at the same time, though. On the way home, Dad told me that someone at church had told him they don't want me helping with Sunday school any more after I'm deaf. I felt totally gutted.

Whatever

Mum told me Sally is coming for dinner. Sally can hear, but she works with deaf people – she knows sign language. Hopefully Sally can put me in touch with some deaf Christians. I'd like that, because I don't know anyone who is deaf. Feel a bit cross that this was arranged without consulting me, though. But whatever. I'm not going to have a future anyway. I want to be a teacher, but how can I be a teacher when I am deaf? How am I going to be anything?

Hard

Took Jasper for a walk and he yanked the lead from my hand! I'm glad he still came back to me.

At church today, Sam said he thinks people should be praying that I don't go deaf. I wish I would be healed, but part of me doesn't think it's what God wants for me. I'm just glad to know people are praying for me – I don't mind what they pray. Mum practised taking notes in the sermon, as she will do that when I am deaf, so I can read. She said it was really hard to keep up. She also said doing the sermon in sign language would be hard.

I think I just make life hard for people.

Wrestling

Mum and I went to visit a lady who has also got NF2. It was the first time I've ever met anyone with NF2, and it was nice to meet someone who understood what it's like. After that, Mum and I took Jasper to the park and let him off the lead for the first time. He was fine, but don't tell the others – they won't be happy we did it without them! Bible study at church was Genesis 22, where Jacob wrestles with God. Jacob was struggling, and it encouraged me that it's OK to struggle. I'm struggling. I feel like I'm wrestling sometimes, trying to be positive but finding it really hard. I helped Pollyanna with her homework last night. I never thought I would wish I had homework again, but I did last night. It would be something to do.

Little d

I am so fed up with writing this diary. As far as I can see, it's of no use at all, but I'll keep at it because I told Mum I would.

Jasper update: let him off the lead again; he was fine.

Sally came round to talk to me about Deaf church. Deaf with a capital D means born deaf; deaf with a little d means lost your hearing later in life. I'm going to be deaf with a little d and I'll be the first 'little d' Christian Sally knows! Mum and Dad and Sally and I were in the front room, talking. Then Sophie came in, then Kirsty, then Pollyanna. They kept talking about themselves, and their homework. We were supposed to be talking about Deaf church! I sometimes find things hard with Sophie: not because of her, we get on really well, but because she's doing all the things I couldn't do. When I was her age, I was in hospital because of NF2. I feel frustrated inside when they all go on about school stuff because I wish I had uni to talk about, but I can't go back at the moment because of the stupid tumours. All I can do is wait to be deaf.

Positive

Went to the hospital today and as Mum and I were walking down the corridor, we saw Clare, my favourite nurse from before! When I saw her, I remembered how she used to get my face all wet when she put my eyedrops in. No idea why I remembered that. Clare said her cousin teaches lipreading with a bit of sign language to help, so it's still English, not a whole new language. Sounds good. I have a feeling that it will help because it seems to me that God must have wanted us to bump into Clare, seeing as it happened in a massive, busy hospital. I'm feeling a bit more positive about being deaf (if that's possible!). I think it helped seeing Sally and bumping into Clare.

Don't know

Had a meeting at church about the Children's Holiday Club. The club will be after my operation, so I don't know if I'll be able to help. I hated not being able to sign up for anything because I don't know how I'll be feeling and I will be deaf.

Went to the cinema with Jodie while she's home for the holidays. Noticed how often the actors have their faces away from the camera. I definitely would not be able to lipread movies!

It's hard to believe I'll be deaf soon.

Explaining

Had a meeting today about how camp went in the summer. I hadn't seen most people since camp, so I had to keep explaining all about the second operation and how I soon won't be able to hear. I felt like I was talking about someone else.

Clare's cousin phoned to sort out my lipreading lessons.

What about them?

The speaker at church today was talking about the time in the Bible, in John 21, when Peter was with Jesus. They were walking along together on the beach, talking about Peter's life, when Peter saw his friend further down the beach: 'What about John, Jesus? What's happening with him?' And Jesus said, 'Don't worry about him, you just follow me.' I feel a bit like Peter, looking at other people, and all they are doing, and all they have got. It reminded me to try to focus on God, not other people.

What?!

When we were walking the dog today, Mum told me that it's not fair on my sisters to keep blocking things out and that they feel they can't talk about things because I don't talk about things.

Maybe they don't know I do, because I talk to you in this diary?

I told Mum I would talk to them and let them know that it's OK with me to talk about how they feel. Mum also told me that I should share how I'm feeling with the rest of the family.

I have to change the way I'm coping with things so that the others will be able to cope better? What?! And anyway, I don't really know how I'm feeling, except that my life is a nightmare I want to wake up from.

Told Mum I'm a bit envious of Sophie doing all the things I'd have liked to do at her age. Mum explained that it's good for Sophie to be doing things I never did. I thought that was a bit insensitive, but I suppose Mum's right.

Sally came round with two of her friends who are deaf. One of them prayed in sign language and it was beautiful.

Sally also brought some information about brainstem implants. I still can't decide whether to have one or not. I'm not sure if I want to be halfway between two communities (deaf and hearing), but then again, it might help with lipreading. And it's not as though the implant will stop me being deaf. But what if it doesn't work? What's it like being deaf, anyway? I don't know what to do.

Apparently the Deaf church Sally told me about has a Sunday school. Perhaps, one day, I'll be able to help out at that. I hope so. At least I'd be doing something.

Boring

I told the story at the children's club at church. It went fine. I watched *Pride and Prejudice*. This entry is really boring, I can't think of anything else to put, so I'm going to read my book now!

Keeping music

Met Clare's cousin today. She's really nice, and we are going to learn sign language with her.

She said I'll still be able to play the piano and flute after the operation because I'll be able to 'hear' the notes through vibrations in my fingers. I've been dreading losing music when I lose my hearing, but I might not lose music after all! I really hope I don't. Aunty Jane phoned and said that TJ has been practising his spellings in sign language.

Wow!

Mum showed me some money that she'd found in an envelope addressed to her and Dad. We don't know who it's from. I thought that kind of thing only happened in books, or to other people, not to us! I've been worrying about how we'll pay for sign language lessons and stuff, and Mum just keeps saying, 'God will provide.' Shows what little faith I have had. Wow!

I think that, by this need for an operation, God is telling me to rely on him. To be honest, I do rely a bit on what I can do as well as on God, but when I lose my hearing, I don't think I'll be able to do anything. I'll have nothing to rely on. I do need to learn to rely on God more.

Teacher

How weird is this. I helped at a children's club at a different church today, and one of the children's mum is the teacher I had when I was 5!

It made me realize again how much I want to be a teacher, but I know that's impossible. How can I work with children if I can't even hear them talking to me? I did lots of talking and listening today. Seeing my old teacher also made me wish I was 5 again: no worries, and definitely not even knowing I had NF2.

I must have had NF2 when I was 5, though, because I was born with it. I was born with a body that would grow tumours. That's so bizarre. I'm glad 5-year-old me didn't know what would happen to me.

Poorly

I don't feel very well today. I never feel very well now, but it's worse today.

I also feel bad that there is so much in this diary about being deaf and poorly. Thank you for still reading!

Butterflies

Went to a concert hall this evening for Christian Praise. Christian Praise happens every year and has bands and singing and different people speaking. It's great, but this was the last time I'll go to a big Christian event when I can actually hear what's happening.

At the end, a man said anyone could go to the front and get prayer for healing. I always get butterflies (not stitches!) in my tummy when that happens, and I feel a bit sick. I do want to be healed, and I do want a life without tumours. So why do you think I feel that maybe God doesn't want to heal me? I'm confused.

Bucket list

Mum phoned and booked tickets for a concert at the Royal Albert Hall in London. I'm so excited! It's one of the things I want to do before I lose my hearing. Kind of like a bucket list. People write bucket lists of things they want to do before they die. A bucket list is a good way to describe it because when I am deaf, my life will be over.

Another thing on my bucket list is: go to see a Shakespeare play at Stratford-upon-Avon. I love going there. Dad says we'll be able to get a box, too! That means special seats. I hope we can see *Richard II* (its real name is *The Life and Death of King Richard the Second*). It's my favourite of Shakespeare's plays. Did you know, he wrote more than thirty plays? His plays had drums to make noise like thunder, and special effects like trap doors on stage, and smoke, and wires lifting actors up. One special effect was a cannon, which is like a big gun, and once it accidentally set fire to the roof and burned the theatre down! Whoops.

Wonky or not?

Saw Dr Dentist Chair today. He said that if I have the brainstem implant, they'll need to remove the whole tumour, which means my face will probably go wonky (he didn't say 'wonky', but that's what he meant). If I don't have the implant, they can just remove some of the tumour and hopefully save my face, like they did last time. I will still be deaf, though.

I don't know what to do. How am I supposed to decide? I should be making decisions about jobs and life, not about my face going wonky.

I want to say 'save the facial nerve so my face isn't wonky', but people who've lost their hearing say they'd do anything to get even some of it back. But the implant is not like real hearing. Most people like me lose most of their hearing as the tumour grows, so they know what deafness is. My hearing is perfect, even though the tumour is massive, so I have no idea what being deaf is like. I'm really scared.

What would you choose? Face or implant?

NF2 means I can't have a good life because I'm ill all the time and I've got tumours everywhere. People say God has a plan for our lives, but it's hard to see what the plan is for my life. I can't wait for my life to be over and to get to heaven.

Plans

I've been thinking about plans. If I am just deaf, maybe God could have a plan, but if my facial nerve goes too, I can't see that he could have any plan for me at all.

Psalm 46:10

We're going away for half-term tomorrow. I'm really looking forward to it, but I keep thinking about how it'll be my last holiday where I can hear. I hate that my hearing – or not hearing – just takes over everything these days.

I got a letter from Ruth today. She put a sticker on it which said 'Be still and know that I am God' . . . it's from Psalm 46. Is God trying to tell me something? I know 'still' in this verse means sort of quiet inside. I'm not quiet inside, because soon my ears will be quiet forever, and it's all I can think about. Maybe God is saying that remembering 'he is God' will help me be still and quiet and peaceful inside. That verse keeps cropping up everywhere: at Christian Praise, on a card from Great-aunt Flora, on my calendar and now on this letter. Maybe God's trying to tell me something?

Asking questions

Holiday was great, and I decided I was not writing this diary on holiday! But back to reality now.

85

The Health Authority have agreed to pay for me to have a brainstem implant, but only if the operation is done in Manchester, not Nottingham. That means someone other than Mr Taylor (and Dr Dentist Chair) gets near my head. That scares me, even if Manchester do have the top NF2 surgeon in the country. I still haven't even decided whether to have an ABI anyway. When I see Mr Taylor on Thursday, I'll ask him again whether the ABI increases the risk to my face. I know it does because they'll remove the whole tumour, but if I keep asking, maybe the answer will change?

Free time

Mr Taylor's secretary phoned today to cancel the appointment on Thursday, because he wants me to have another brain scan before I see him. I hate those brain scans!

I'm glad about the appointment being cancelled. Mum wants to get a definite date for the operation, but I think, if I had a definite date, it would be like having a horrible countdown. I sometimes count down the days until a holiday, or something special, but I don't want to count down to being deaf.

Now I have some free time – no hospital or operation yet! – and I can go and visit Aunty Jane, and maybe go to see Jodie at her university on the way.

Shopping

Had a great time with Jodie. We
went shopping and she sorted
me out with some new clothes. Some things never change.
I'm rubbish at shopping, always have been. I don't know how
Jo puts up with me!

I had a brilliant time in Newcastle with Aunty Jane, too.
Highlights:

Going to see *Hamlet.*

Going to see *The Prime of Miss Jean Brodie.*

I love going to the theatre, and we had the best seats *both* times!

I spent most of the week with Aunty Jane, as the others were
at work/school. It reminded me of when I was little and I
used to spend a lot of time with Aunty Jane, just her and me.
Maybe that's why we are so close now.

I listened to TJ read. Won't be able to do that soon.

We listened to a recording of JJ and TJ's school concert.
JJ sang a solo! Aunty Jane got the recording especially, because
soon I won't be able to hear; no one said anything as we
listened, but we all knew it was 'now or never' for me to hear
them singing. Actually, now or never to hear them doing
anything.

See, everything is about hearing. Before, I never even thought about hearing! You don't, do you? You just do it.

Ballgowns

We went to see Handel's *Messiah* tonight (more hearing). Grandma and Grandad take us every year, and they always buy sweets for us.

It was a brilliant performance. My favourite song in it – though they're nearly all my favourites! – is 'I know that my redeemer liveth'. It's in the *Messiah* but it was first written in an old version of the Bible called the King James Version (KJV), Job 19:25. Sometimes it's hard to understand what the KJV is saying, because it's written in old English. 'I know that my redeemer liveth' is what Job said, but I would say: 'I know that Jesus – my Saviour – is alive.' The soloist sang the song beautifully tonight. The soloists wear gorgeous dresses, a bit like Cinderella wears when she goes to the ball! As they sang, I kept thinking, 'This is the last time I will hear the *Messiah* live.'

Ruined

Sophie keeps talking about learning to drive. I am trying not to be envious, but I'm not doing very well! I wish she'd stop going on about it. It also reminds me of all the plans I made. I was going to learn to drive when I was 17. Instead I was on a life support machine. *Stupid NF2 ruins everything.*

Sitting around

Found out yesterday that there's been a mix-up, so I probably won't get my scan, let alone have the operation, until the New Year. I'm glad to have the operation and being deaf even further away, but I could have done another semester at uni. I wouldn't have had to sit around doing nothing.

At the prayer meeting at church, people prayed that I would be healed if it's what God wants. I think that's a good way to pray. I hope it is what God wants! But I'm still not sure it is . . .

Stuff

Mum and Dad went to see a geneticist today, and they didn't even tell me they were going. I can't believe that! The geneticist wants to try to work out why I've got NF2. I don't know why they need to know; it's not as if how I got NF2 makes any difference, I've still got it in my body.

Mum and Dad and my sisters still need to be tested to see if they have NF2. I really, really hope they haven't. I would hate it if they do have NF2, and had to go through the stuff I go through.

I don't want it

Mum got upset today. She doesn't want me to have the operation. I don't want to have it, either. I don't want to be deaf. Mostly I try to pretend my life is not happening to me.

Charades

Went to the Deaf church today, for the first time, with Mum. The speaker was from America, and sign language is different over there, so we weren't the only ones who didn't understand him. In the end it was like we were playing charades – everyone trying to work out what his actions meant!

Purple jacket

It was Sophie's presentation evening at school tonight, and I lent her my purple jacket to wear, even though it's my favourite. She promised not to go out in it afterwards, but then she did. I'm so mad at her!

Too ill

I'm feeling really fed up. What am I going to do after my operation? I know there are deaf teachers, but a deaf teacher with NF2 who can't even speak sign language properly? I don't think so.

Sunday school is changing and now you have to be able
to commit yourself to it *every week*. I can't do that because
sometimes I feel too ill. No more Sunday school for me, then.

Every Christmas, all the helpers at Discoverers put on a play
for the children. I was the angel this year and had to dress
up in white, with silver tinsel on my head. The tinsel was my
halo, but it kept falling off!

Still can't believe I'll be deaf soon.

No friends

I wish I had some friends. My friends have all moved away,
or I never see them in classes and stuff now. I don't even see
Jodie. Mum thinks I'm being silly, and she said that of course
I've got friends. I think she's trying to play down the things
that I find hard so that I don't find them so difficult. But I do
find them hard, and that's the truth.

Squeamish

I had a tiny plug thing put in my eyelid at the hospital today,
to try to stop my eye being so dry and sore. I'm getting used
to hospital things, but I will *never* get used to having my eyes
operated on. Eyes make me squeamish.

Went to a Christmas carol concert this evening. It was good and I've decided to just try to not keep thinking, 'This is the last time . . .'

The worst

I felt ill last night. Really bad headache, and I felt sick, and I ached all over. People say deafness is not the worst thing about NF2, and I'm beginning to understand what they mean. I felt so rough.

Special present

Tonight I played my flute in a Christmas concert. It was the last concert I will ever play in. I feel really sad tonight; playing in concerts has been part of my life for as long as I can remember. My flute is really special, as well. It was a present from my family.

1999

Beach

New Year's Day today. We're staying at Aunty Jane's, near the sea. I went to the beach with my cousins. It was freezing cold! We got soaked when the tide came in – just like we were big kids! It was nice pretending I was little again, because then I didn't know about NF2.

Waiting to be deaf

I'm getting more and more scared about the operation. I have my scan in four days' time. I know I need to make a decision about whether to have the implant or not, but I still don't know. How am I supposed to make such a big decision?

Granny said today that she didn't think God would let my facial nerve go. I hope she's right. I don't want a wonky face.

It's really hard not knowing about when the operation will be, and all the delays. I can't make any plans to do anything; I'm just waiting to be deaf. How rubbish is that?

Talking

I saw a psychiatrist today. Dr Margaret is deaf. She lost her hearing, but not because of NF2. So she's deaf with a little d: she grew up hearing. I saw her because people say that one day I'll be deaf. I still don't think I will, though, not deep inside, even though at the same time I'm scared that I will be. That doesn't make sense, does it? It's just that I am not a deaf person, and I cannot imagine being one. The reason I agreed to see Dr Margaret is because she's deaf. Back when Dr Dentist Chair first told me I would be deaf, Mum asked him what support I would have, and that's why I saw Dr Margaret. She's really nice.

It is just me and her, and we talk, and I can ask her what it's like being deaf. I only ask in an interested way. It won't happen to me, but I can still be interested. She's easy to talk to, and we have lots of laughs. It's nice to know that when people go deaf, they can still be happy and have a life. She's not got NF2 as well, though. I'm going to keep seeing Dr Margaret every week.

Confused

I saw Mr Taylor today, after seeing Dr Dentist Chair last week. But now I'm totally confused. It's like some weird mystery game where I don't know the rules.

Dentist Chair told me that *both* tumours in my head have grown massively, that there was hardly any chance of saving my facial nerve, and that the operation to make me deaf would have to be done soon.

Mr Taylor told me that the tumour they operated on before has not grown, but new ones have grown around it. He said that there is a good chance of stopping my face being wonky, and that the operation needed to be in the next six months.

Talk about a rollercoaster, and I still don't know which doctor is right!

Failure

Sophie had a parents' evening today, and was told she should get an A in music. At the same stage, I was told I'd get an A in

English, but then I found out I have NF2 and I missed a lot of school and I didn't get an A. I'm still gutted about that. I can just about cope with having NF2 (maybe), but I can't cope with it turning me into a failure. And it already is turning me into a failure.

Scared

I saw Dr Margaret today and we talked about how scared I am about my face being wonky, even though we are supposed to be talking about deaf stuff! She made me feel that maybe I could cope with a wonky face. I still hope it doesn't happen, though.

I've realized why I don't like telling people I am deaf in one ear. It's because of the reason why I am – NF2. Even if they don't ask why, and I am the only one that knows, it's still rubbing it in, to me. I only really talk about it to you in this diary.

Different

I've been thinking about the future, and how I won't have children. Maybe God wants something different for me?

Not doing well

I thought I was doing quite well but I'm not. I'm just back from a big Christian festival – loads of singing and music and bands. It just reminded me of all I'm going to lose. The festival was the last big thing I had planned, really, and now it's over the next thing will be the operation. I am petrified. I'm feeling a bit dead inside. It would be better if I just die. I'm seeing Dr Margaret tomorrow; maybe I'll tell her about this stuff.

1 a.m.: Can't sleep. I want to get my feelings and emotions about NF2 out, but I don't know how. I want to but I can't. I just feel hollow inside, like I'm not all here.

My name is missing

An email came through with the programme for a children's event at church; there's so much to do! Everyone's name is down to do something, except mine. I wish people would let me do stuff.

Splat!

I ended up doing 'Splat the Rat' game at the event. It's where you have a long tube, put a bean bag in the top, and someone has to try to hit the bean bag with a bat when it comes out. They don't know when it will come out, though, so it's quite tricky! I really want to be involved in the new Sunday school that's starting, but I know I can't. People don't want me to, anyway.

Questions

It says in Psalm 55:22: 'Give your worries to the Lord. He will take care of you.' Helpful verse for me to read today as I go to

Manchester to see the top doctor – sorry, professor – in two days' time. I'm seeing Professor Ramsden to talk about whether to have the ABI when I have surgery. I'm so nervous. What if he gives me a date for the op? How am I going to cope, not hearing for the rest of my life? And will he agree with Dentist Chair or Mr Taylor about when the operation needs to be done?

Shock

I don't even know where to start. Professor Ramsden didn't want to talk about implants. He was amazed I could still hear on one side, because normally when the tumour grows, it makes people deaf even before surgery. But I can hear perfectly on that side, so the professor didn't want to operate until he really had to, because he didn't want to make me deaf. I'm in shock. After all this worrying, I'm told I won't be deaf! I need an operation on my already-deaf side instead.

Still confused

Spoke to Dr Dentist Chair, who said I need the operation soon and there's a 'very high risk' of my facial nerve being damaged. Professor Ramsden said 50 per cent chance. I'm seeing Mr Taylor soon to discuss things with him, too.

Oh, and apparently *I'm* supposed to decide if I want Professor Ramsden or Dentist Chair/Mr Taylor to do the operation. How should I know?

God

I'm just reading in Deuteronomy 6:5 about how important it is to love God with all our hearts. If I'm being honest, I haven't loved God with *all* my heart.

Today at church someone told me that she'd been thinking about the women in the Bible who went to the tomb to find Jesus' body after he died. They worried all the way there about how they were going to move the stone from the front of the tomb, but when they got there God had it all under control and everything was fine.

Healing

It's 6.13 a.m. and I can't sleep. There are these healing meetings happening, and two people have told me I should go. I don't know what to do. It's not that I don't want to be healed. If I could go back to 'life before NF2' I would. But is healing me what God wants? And what if I go but I'm not healed? I'll feel like I'm letting people down.

Damaged

I saw Mr Taylor, and he said he would operate on the same side of my brain as before, if I wanted him to. I decided to stick with him, not go to Professor Ramsden. I know Mr Taylor. Mr Taylor said the left tumour has not actually grown back, but others have grown around it, on my swallow nerve and my facial nerve. If my swallow nerve is damaged in surgery, I'll be on a feeding tube for the rest of my life. If my face nerve goes, I might be blind. My face probably will be damaged this time. I begged Mr Taylor to take my hearing instead. If my face is damaged, my life is over. Everyone will keep staring. I hate it when people look at me. When I first saw Dr Dentist Chair, I said to him I'd rather lose my hearing than my face, and he said losing hearing is worse. I'm not so sure about that. Anyway, Mr Taylor can't take hearing instead of face, so that's that. Nineteen years old and needing brain surgery for the second time, which will maybe mean I can't swallow or see, and with a wonky face. The little bit of 'fight' left in me has gone. I can't be positive any more.

Smile

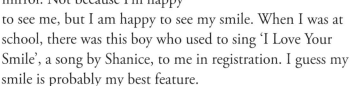

I keep smiling at myself in the mirror. Not because I'm happy to see me, but I am happy to see my smile. When I was at school, there was this boy who used to sing 'I Love Your Smile', a song by Shanice, to me in registration. I guess my smile is probably my best feature.

I read a verse in the Bible, in 1 Samuel 16:7, 'People look at the outside of a person, but the Lord looks at the heart.' That made me feel a bit better. If my face is damaged, other people will stare at it, but God won't. He doesn't mind what I look like.

What can I do?

Sue walked past me at church and said that, as she did, an old song, 'There's a Work for Jesus' about how Jesus has something for everyone to do popped into her head, and she wondered why. I wonder too. I can't do anything, except grow tumours. It's hard as well not to look at other people and compare their lives to mine. I wish I had been able to carry on with uni.

Stupid

I hate it when I can't hear people properly when they talk on my deaf side, and so they have to speak louder and slower. Feel so stupid.

Smile?

Last time I saw Dr Margaret she said to email her if I need to. I thought 'I won't need to', but now there isn't time, I wish I had emailed her. Today is Friday. My operation is on Monday. I'm going into hospital in three days' time. It's soon, and I'm scared. I keep thinking of when I calmly looked at my brain scan pictures with Professor Ramsden – I don't think I could look at them calmly now. Will I have a smile after Monday?

Dribble

I woke up after the surgery. It took twelve hours again, but no need for more operations or intensive care this time. When I woke up, Mum was there, just like she always is. She said, 'They got all of the tumour out, Em,' and I didn't even have to ask her if my face was wonky.

I knew it was.

Half my face wouldn't move. Can you imagine that? I dribbled and couldn't stop myself. Someone gave me a drink, and I spilled it down me because my mouth wouldn't close around the cup.

What a baby.

At least I'm not blind, I suppose.

Staring

Sophie came with Mum to visit me in hospital today, and when she saw me trying to drink with a straw, she just stared at me. I hated that. I don't want anyone looking at me. Ever.

Sophie is learning to drive now. She is 17. It's weird to think what happened to me when I was 17. Sophie really wants to be able to drive to the hospital and visit me. I want her to as well.

Mirror

A nurse asked me to look in a mirror. I said no. I don't even look in the mirror over the sink when I wash my hands! I look away from it. The nurses keep suggesting I look, but I won't.

I know I look awful. I never want to see myself.

Hideous

I'm going home today, but before I do, the nurse said I have to look in a mirror. Yes, that's right: have to. She brought a mirror to my bed. I had a quick look, then put it facing downwards.

My face looks hideous, like half of it has slipped down. My eye droops, my nose droops, my mouth droops. I just hope I can get from the car to the house without seeing anyone, then I'm never leaving the house again. I'll have to see my sisters, I know, but I really wish they didn't have to see me like this. They've had to see so much, and I'm their big sister; I should be looking after them, not scaring them.

Oh yes, I forgot to write this: my sisters had their tests for NF2. I'm not really sure why they waited, but the geneticist told them they could choose when to have the test, and they chose to wait.

None of them has got NF2! Even Pollyanna. *None* of them. Mum and Dad haven't, either. It's just me. I am so relieved. Mum seems a bit sad about it. I don't know why.

Baby food

I got into the house without seeing anyone, and I've not gone out since. I stay in, mostly playing the piano and eating baby food. I can't chew now, because of my face. It won't move, or keep chewy food in. Loads of things are too hard for me to eat now. I can't even eat egg sandwiches! So Mum mushes all my food down. She makes it look as nice as possible, but it's still baby food.

Early days

I can't play the flute now. My lips won't make the right shape to blow across the instrument. All I can play is the low notes, which don't need my lips to be so tight, but I can't play them very well. Maybe things will get better. Do you think they will? Everyone keeps telling me it's early days, but it feels like early days have been going on for a long time to me.

Dizzy

Felt frustrated today. I tried to prove to Mum that I'm not too dizzy after the operation now, but I totally failed. I tried to stand up from a chair, and I fell over!

Someone else

The photo arrived in the post today.

Before I had 'the face' operation, Mum booked for me to have a photo shoot at a studio. When I got there, someone did my hair and make-up. I never wear make-up, but I did that day. It was funny afterwards: I phoned Mum to pick me up, and then waited outside the studio. She drove past, looking for me, but she didn't recognize me! She didn't stop and had to circle the block, but thankfully she realized it was me second time round.

I opened the envelope, which was brown just like the envelope that had my brain scans in when I first saw Dr Dentist Chair, and pulled out a big photo of me. It should have been like looking in a mirror, but it wasn't.

The new me stared at the old me. The old me could smile.

Do you ever wish you were someone else? Well, the new me wished I was the old me.

Worried

It's been a month since my operation and today I read my Bible for the first time since I had surgery. I think God prompted me to or something

because I haven't wanted to before. I'm just so angry at the moment, about how little I can do. My balance is rubbish, my face is wonky, I can't play the flute. I read today in 2 Corinthians 12:9: 'When you are weak, then my power is made perfect in you.' If it's weakness God needs, he's got that in me! I can't do anything.

I don't like being so weak, but if it means more of God's power, maybe that's a good thing? It's hard, though. I hate not being able to do anything. I'm worried about the future, too. I'm just about coping now, but NF2 is a nightmare. It's like it has a mind of its own, with tumours popping up all over.

What if more tumours grow massive? I can't cope with having operations for the rest of my life.

2000

New

A new year. A new millennium. A new me without tumours? I wish. A new me who is totally deaf? I hope not.

Wishing

Mum was talking about my friends graduating from university soon.

Went and lay on my bed and listened to music.

I felt gutted; I wish it was me graduating, too. I wish I didn't have my life taken over by NF2. I wish I had more interesting things to write about. I'm glad I can talk to you.

Piano

It's been months now, and no improvement in my face. It's as wonky and hideous as ever. I can sort of play the flute at church, but an octave lower, and I play quietly. On purpose. I never used to do that.

I've started being a bit braver and going out of the house more than just to church. I'm doing some voluntary things, and I still help with the children's club at church on Tuesdays. I think I'm allowed to because I didn't go deaf. The children are great. Adults find it awkward when they see my face, they don't know what to say, but the children just ask, 'What happened to your face?' then they carry on with whatever they are doing. I play the piano for singing time (my wonky face doesn't stop me playing the piano); I took over from my friend when she went to university. We sing songs about God, and the world, and how God made us all. I know he made me. I'm glad I know it, but I still don't think about Psalm 139 too much.

I can't go back to university. Well, I mean, I could, but I don't have the confidence. Not with my face looking like it does.

Practising

I've decided to start having piano lessons
again. I feel a bit confident with just one
other person. I'm going to practise this time
round. If my teacher thought I was good
even without proper practising, hopefully I
can make up for it now and get better!

Normal

Scan time again. My tumour on my hearing side has grown,
but no need to operate.

For now, anyway, said Mr Taylor.

I have a sort of hearing aid. It's like two hearing aids joined
by a wire. The wire goes behind my head and the hearing aids
go on my ears. It's called a crossover hearing aid. The sound
from my deaf side is supposed to go along the wire and my
hearing side will hear it. I don't like it, it just confuses me, and
anyway, it looks silly. I don't wear it much.

Because the tumour on my hearing side is growing, the
doctors want to get me ready for being deaf, so I've got to go
to see a hearing therapist.

I won't be deaf, though, will I? I won't. But it's hard to keep
believing that now. I saw the scan, with the big white lump of

tumour squashing my head. How did looking at brain scans become normal for me?

So I've got to go to see a hearing therapist.

Cinderella

The hearing therapist is nice and told me things I'd never have thought of. When I lose my hearing (I don't like saying 'deaf', it makes it more real), I will try to lipread people, and I need to make sure they are in the right place. So if a light is behind them, it puts their face in shadow and I won't be able to see their lips. We tried it and she's right! I'd never have thought of that, would you?

Another thing I have to do now is ask people to say something to me without using their voice, so I can try to understand. It's a bit like a game! But I don't want to win, because I don't want to lipread, because I don't want to be deaf.

Pollyanna reads *Cinderella* to me with no voice. The ballgown pictures in the book look like the people who sing in the *Messiah*! After every sentence, Pollyanna stops and I tell her what she just said, to see if I got it right. It's like role reversal.

I used to go into her school and help her and her friends with reading.

Roller skates

My church is going to put on a musical! It's called *Snakes and Ladders* by Roger Jones. It's the story of the Bible, so it starts right at the beginning with Adam and Eve, then carries on with different characters, like Moses and Abraham and Mary. I'm going to be in it. I wasn't sure at first; it will be a big deal for me to get up on stage. I try not to let people see me, so going on stage doesn't really make sense! But I love musicals. I've seen *Phantom of the Opera, Starlight Express, Joseph and the Amazing Technicolor Dreamcoat, Les Misérables.* They're great. In *Starlight Express,* the people in it were on roller skates! I saw that one a few years ago with my choir because we were singing songs from it. Like 'Light at the End of the Tunnel' by Richard Stilgoe and Andrew Lloyd Webber. There's not a light at the end of my tunnel. It's just getting darker and darker. I'm still pretending deafness isn't coming, but I know it's waiting for me. Maybe that's why I want to sing at church. I'm singing a duet with Kirsty, called 'Engraved Upon My Palms', about how God will never forget us. I don't think he's forgotten about me; I just hope he's not forgotten that I am not a deaf person and never will be.

Argument

I'm glad I don't have to be Eve in the musical. When I was 14, Jodie and I were helping with a children's holiday club at a church away from home, and we all slept in different houses, hosted by church people. At the end of one day, the team realized someone needed to act as Eve the following day. They said either Jodie or me, we could decide between us. When Jo and I got to our bedroom, she said, 'I'm not doing it.' I said, 'I'm not.' We argued all night and, in the morning, we were still friends but I was Eve. Jodie lent me her shirt, and helped me stick leaves all over it, but I still had to be Eve. I always knew it would end up being me. Jodie said she knew it would be me, too, because I always say yes. Well, saying 'no' obviously doesn't work, does it?

Dark times

More brain scan results tomorrow.
I've just read Psalm 139:11,12.

I don't know why I read the psalm I
don't like to think about! But these verses are good. I know I didn't write them, but I pretend the 'I' is me, and I know the 'you' is God:

I could say, 'The darkness will hide me. The light around me will turn into night. But even the darkness is not dark to you. The night is as light as the day. Darkness and light are the same to you.'

Scan results are scary; they're never good news. Every time I'm told about tumours that show up, and every time I feel like I've been punched. I'm glad God knows my dark times. They are not dark to him, but I wish I didn't have to know them.

Hearing

I have to go to see Professor Ramsden again. Mr Taylor says the tumour that will make me deaf is huge now. But I can still hear from that side. I can hear fine! I'm not too worried.

I don't think they will need to operate. Hopefully Professor Ramsden will leave it longer and realize that I am not a deaf person and never will be.

Worst choice ever

'Your hearing or your life.'

OK, so Professor Ramsden actually said, 'Either we operate and you lose your hearing, or we don't operate and you lose your life,' but it means my hearing or my life. What sort of a choice is that? So the tumour will either kill me or kill my hearing. My life should have a 'Beware, tumours kill' sign over it.

It didn't cross my mind to say 'no operation', and I'm going to get a letter with a date for surgery. That means I will know the exact date when I will lose my hearing.

Rainbows

When Mum, Dad and I walked out of the hospital, it was raining, and we got soaked just running to the car.

I didn't mind. I was feeling rubbish anyway. Who cares about a bit of rain when they've just been told that even though they are not a deaf person, they soon will be?

I was staring out of the car window at the rain running down it from the grey sky, when I saw a rainbow. It was amazing, and I felt a little bit better. I know God puts rainbows in the sky to remind us that he will look after us. They're a sign of his promise. I still know God will look after me, but I'm really scared about being deaf.

As we drove home, I saw another rainbow. Then another. They just kept coming! God kept reminding me of his promise! Even in the rain, there was something beautiful to see.

I feel like I'm being rained on. My life is hard and grey and horrid. Maybe I can find rainbows in the rain? I'm going to look for something good every day. #everydayrainbows

What do I want to hear?

I'm making a list of things I want to hear before I can't hear. I think I really will lose my hearing this time (but I wrote that in a tiny whisper; I don't want to say it out loud):

1. Music (that will happen because I have music on all the time).
2. Voices of my family (that will hopefully happen, but some live in Australia, and it depends on how long I'm allowed to

stay on the phone to them. Normally we can't stay on long, because it's expensive).

3. Go to Menorca.
4. A live performance of Handel's *Messiah* (will probably happen because we go every year, just before Christmas, which is only a few weeks away now).
5. A play at the Royal Shakespeare Theatre (RST) in Stratford.

Number 5 reminds me of when my family and I went to the RST last time we thought I would soon be deaf. I wanted to see *Richard II* then, but the only play on was *A Comedy of Errors*!

#everydayrainbows: that's a great memory

Won't be able to

I got a date for surgery: 15 November. I won't be able to go to Handel's *Messiah*. I won't be able to be in the musical at church, either.

Bad news about Number 5. *Richard II* is not on at the RST. But that's not the really bad news. The really bad news is about *The Secret Garden*. *The Secret Garden* was written by someone called Frances Hodgson Burnett and is one of my favourite books. It's all about children finding a hidden garden that has been locked up for a long time. The children look after the garden and make it beautiful again. There is going to be a musical of *The Secret Garden*, at the RST! But it opens on 13 November. That's the day I have to go to hospital to get ready for my operation. That's why it's bad news.

Bad news about Number 3 as well. Professor Ramsden says I'm not allowed to fly, so we can't go to Menorca. I hate that my NF2 is stopping my family from doing stuff, as well as me. We're going to have a holiday in the UK instead, but it's not the same.

It's hard to find a rainbow today.

Invitation

Mum wrote to the Royal Shakespeare Theatre and explained, and guess what?! They phoned and invited us to go to watch the final dress rehearsal of *The Secret Garden*! That'll be just like the real thing. And it's on 10 November, so I can go.

#everydayrainbows: my mum

Family

Instead of Menorca, we are staying in a conference centre not far from home. My grandparents, great-aunt, aunt, uncle and cousins are here, too. It's great; there are so many of us but we all fit in fine. There's no one else here, so we get the place to ourselves, which means we never have to queue for the pool table! I know this will be the last time I see my cousins when I can hear them. I'm trying not to think about that.

#everydayrainbows: I beat my cousin at pool

Candles

Today everyone decided to walk from the centre into the local village. I can't do that – my balance is rubbish again, and I get really tired – so I stayed behind with a book. I couldn't concentrate on my book, though. Why can't I go and do things? They'll be off having a great time, and I'm stuck here. When I heard them come back, I didn't go and say hello, but my sisters came straight to find me. They wanted to show me a present Dad had bought me. A candlestick. I love candles! And I don't need to hear them. I felt bad for being so grumpy.

#everydayrainbows: my dad

Nearly November

It's nearly November now.

November

1 November. Fifteen days to go.

Stay awake

I have to go to hospital on the 13th, and stay until the operation. So the night before surgery, I'll be in hospital. Sleeping will be a waste of time. I'll be asleep for the next twelve hours anyway, on an operating table, but more importantly, why would I waste my last night of hearing by being asleep?

So I need to choose what music I'll listen to. It's the last music I will ever hear. I'm trying really hard to find a rainbow.

#everydayrainbows: I have lots of music to choose from

No!

I am not having a foreign body in my head! I'm not. Well, it's called an ABI, not a 'foreign body', but I think foreign body describes it better. I had enough trouble trying to decide before, and I can't go through all that again. It's Professor Ramsden's idea to give me one this time, even though he said he wouldn't last time. He tried to explain about it, but it's really confusing. See if this makes sense to you:

In surgery, he wants to put this thing in my brain, attached to wires that will link to a hearing aid-type thing. And then I might hear sound after I'm deaf, but I might not. Or maybe, rather than hearing, it will make my arm twitch, or somewhere else twitch. But it might not work at all. I'd be only the eleventh person in Europe to have it, so the professor must not have had much practise! And even if it works, which I don't suppose it will, it won't be like proper hearing. It will be beeps and buzzes. Who wants beeps and buzzes all the time? I can't even imagine what it's like not to hear, let alone just have beeps and buzzes. What use would they be? And I'll have this thing in my head.

See why I don't want it? Mum really wants me to have it but it won't be in her head, will it? I'm not having it.

Fireworks

Bonfire night. I love fireworks! My favourites are the ones that float and sparkle like stars. I don't like the bang-y ones, or the screech-y ones so much. That's good, I guess, because soon I won't be able to hear them anyway.

#everydayrainbows: my family and friends helped me go to a firework display

Stop the clock

Time goes really quickly when you don't want it to. I wish I could stop time. If it stopped right now, I'd always be able to hear. In the Bible, someone called Joshua prayed that the sun would stand still until his army had won the battle. You can read about it in Joshua 10. Dad told me sun standing still means time would stop, like the clock would stop. And it did. Joshua won!

I feel like I'm in an NF2 battle, and I have to fight it, every day. But time doesn't stop for me, and I'm not winning this battle. I'm losing it. Big time. Back when Dr Dentist Chair told me I'd be deaf one day, he told me losing my hearing would be worse than having my facial nerve damaged. I didn't think he could be right, especially after my face went wonky. I hate my face. But what if losing my hearing is even worse?

It's the 10th today. This afternoon, we are going to see the dress rehearsal of *The Secret Garden*.

#everydayrainbows: this afternoon, I'm going to forget about the operation

Brilliant

The Secret Garden musical was amazing. Someone met us at the door of the theatre and took us onto the stage to see all the scenery and props. People kept coming to say hello, and talk to us, and then we were shown to red velvet seats. Apart from the theatre team, it was only us in the whole theatre. Someone turned the lights down, and the production started. Before long, someone called Lucy came and sat with me. She had composed the music for the show, and she stayed with me the whole time. She was really nice, and she knew her music was some of the last I'd ever hear. In five days' time, I'd be deaf. Well, four now, because this happened yesterday. Lucy was really interested in me and my story, but mostly we talked about music. When we did, I almost forgot that soon all my music will be gone.

#everydayrainbows: Lucy

Thinking

I've been thinking and thinking about what music to listen to on my last night of hearing. I've always liked classical best, but there's loads of music I like. I never thought I'd be choosing the last bit of music to listen to, though. How do I choose? What would you choose? I've decided on Handel's *Messiah*, but for now I'm listening to as much music as I can. I want to stuff my head full of music. Maybe I'll still remember it, even when I can't hear?

Little-J

I'm going to hospital tomorrow. My bag is all packed with my pyjamas and dressing gown and slippers and toothbrush. I've put Little-J in, too. I love Little-J. Little-J is a beanie toy dog Aunty Jane gave me because I can't take Jasper into hospital with me. I wish I could.

I've just finished phoning people in my family. Even with the phone call to Australia, I could stay on as long as I wanted! It was strange talking to my cousins for the last time when I've never even seen them. I talked to my aunty over there as well. I saved the hardest phone call for last: to Sophie. She's in Zambia at the moment, having a gap year. When we are together, we never stop talking. Next time we are together, I won't be able to hear her talking. I felt nervous phoning her. At first, it was fine, we just chatted away like we normally do, but then we both suddenly remembered that this was not a normal chat. We couldn't think of anything to say then.

We just held the phones to our ears; silence before silence had come. In the end, I said 'Bye' and she said 'Bye' and that's the last time I will ever hear her voice. Sometimes it's really hard to think of rainbows.

Creaky stairs

Aunty Jane came to stay with Kirsty and Pollyanna, and Mum, Dad and I left the house, got in the car and drove up to Manchester. When I come back to the house, I won't be able to hear. What will that be like? I don't know.

I won't be able to hear the stair creak. When I was little, I always knew that when the stair creaked it meant Mum was on her way up to tell me to stop reading and go to sleep.

Plastic bracelet

In the car on the way to the hospital, we didn't really talk much. There's nothing to say. We had Classic FM on the radio. We seemed to get to the hospital really quickly. The journey normally takes ages.

We went up to the ward, and a nurse showed me to my bed and put a plastic bracelet thing on me. On it is my name, birthday, and if I'm allergic to anything. I'm allergic to Elastoplast and bee stings. Elastoplast makes me red and sore, and bee stings make me swell up. I always think it's funny when they write down that I am allergic to bee stings: it makes me imagine they have bees flying around in the hospital. Some people save their plastic bracelets when they leave hospital, sort of like a souvenir. I don't save mine. I've had so many now, and why would I want to be reminded, anyway?

I feel a bit like a robot, just going through the motions in a life that I don't understand. It shouldn't be my life.

I know people are praying for me. I'm not really praying; I don't know what to pray. It's more like I'm just really aware that God is with me.

Maybe that's enough: #everydayrainbows

Long sleeves

I didn't sleep much last night. It's hard to sleep in hospital when it's so noisy and lights keep flashing. I knew that when I woke up it would be my last day of hearing. This time tomorrow, I will be having my operation. I have to have some tests and things done today and then the nurse said I can go out of the hospital for dinner. I'd better wear long sleeves, so they cover my hospital bracelet.

#everydayrainbows: I can still hear today

Last dinner

I have never felt more alone
in my life. Mum, Dad and
I went out for dinner, to an
Indian restaurant, because I
like Indian food. It was the
last time I will eat while I
can hear. Tomorrow I'll be
'nil by mouth', starting from
midnight tonight. That's
because you're not supposed

to eat before an operation. I think it's in case you want to be
sick in theatre, and the doctors don't want you to be.

Dinner was nice but a bit weird as well. We were trying to
pretend it was just a normal dinner, but we all knew it wasn't.
A funny thing happened: across the restaurant, we saw a table
with some of my doctors eating. I didn't go and say hello; I
don't think they'd want to see me when they are not at work.
And they'll see more than enough of me tomorrow, anyway.
They'll see my brain.

The hospital said I had to be back by 10 p.m., and we went
back as close to 10 p.m. as we could. When we got there,
Mum and Dad couldn't stay on the ward; they had to go to
their hotel.

I sat on my bed and watched them walk away. Then I put my
pyjamas on – my pink ones with white clouds on them – and
climbed into bed; time to listen to Handel's *Messiah*. 'I know

that my redeemer liveth'. Those words are in the *Messiah* and they are in the Bible as well. A man called Job wrote them. He was going through rubbish stuff, and was really ill, but he still knew God was alive and with him. I know it, too. All night, I lay there, cuddling Little-J and listening to Handel's *Messiah* through my headphones. At midnight a nurse came and put a 'nil by mouth' sign by my bed. I hugged Little-J tighter and tried to ignore that sign. I know that my redeemer liveth . . .

#everydayrainbows: Indian food

Teddy bear

At 7 a.m. I took my headphones off. A nurse was standing by my bed, and she told me it was time to go to the bathroom and clean my teeth and put a hospital gown on.

'It's nearly time for theatre.'

When I got back from the bathroom, Mum and Dad were waiting by my bed.

At 8 a.m. someone arrived to push me in my bed to theatre. I was so cold.

Theatre is miles away. Miles of corridors. Mum and Dad walked beside my bed the whole way, one each side. They held my hands.

We came to some doors that said 'theatre' above them. They also said 'no unauthorized access'. That meant only people involved in surgery could go through. I looked at the doors.

When I was 12, I went horse riding every day for a week. There were about ten of us, and a minibus picked us up and took us to the stables. I didn't know anyone, but that was fine, and I loved horse-riding. My horse was called Misty, and I loved him. I tried to keep myself to myself and just stay with Misty, but a couple of the boys still picked on me. I don't know why. One day, when I tried to climb onto the bus, one of them said, 'Shut the door in front of you.' I knew what he meant. Shut the door in front of me so I couldn't get on the bus. He didn't want me there.

I wished I could shut the theatre doors in front of me, so I couldn't go in and get my hearing taken away from me. I didn't want to go in there. But I had to, and the doors would shut in front of Mum and Dad, not in front of me. Mum and Dad couldn't come with me. I was on my own.

'I love you.' That's the last thing I heard them say. Even Dad said it.

The doors shut behind me, and I saw a teddy bear sitting on a cupboard in the room. There wasn't much else in the room, apart from me and doctors.

The doctor put a smelly mask on me and told me to breathe deeply and count backwards from 10.

Ten, nine . . . I don't want to go to sleep

Eight, seven . . . I'm not someone who can't hear

Six, five . . . I know that my redeemer liveth

Bubble

It's like I'm in a bubble and sound can't get through. I look at things that should be making a noise, like a chair scraping on the floor, or someone coughing, but the noise doesn't reach me. I hear

Nothing
At
All.

When people talk to me, I don't know what they are saying. I know I learned a bit of lipreading, but it's different when it's for real. I panic. People talk about me over my head, as if I'm 4 years old or something. Mum does sign language to me, which helps, and people write things down for me. We're still not good at sign language, but it's better than not knowing it at all.

I hate this silence. This time two days ago, I could hear. Now I hear nothing. It's horrid, and I'm scared.

Silence

I know that my redeemer liveth. I do know it. I do. Even in this silent world. #everydayrainbows

Not on my own

#everydayrainbows: I don't need to lipread God! I've never thought of that before. Everyone else, I have to watch their lips moving and try to make sense of it. I get it wrong loads, but God still speaks in my heart, just like before when I was really me and could hear. I don't always know what he's saying but it's really clear at the moment. Ironic or what. Anyway, he's reminding me he's here with me. It helps. This is the worst thing that's ever happened to me, and yet God is here too. He's staying with me.

Out of my room

I had to walk a bit today. After brain surgery, my whole body is weak, and I have to get it going again. Walking was hard, and I shuffled along the corridor in my dressing gown with a Zimmer frame and a big bandage on my head. Still feel like I'm in a bubble. Walking to the bathroom was the first time I came out of my room since I lost my hearing three days ago. I had to go past people; it felt like I was a long way away from them and that I was watching them in a silent movie.

I was glad to get back to my room. I don't normally get my own room in hospital, but Mum told me that the nurses put me here this time because they knew not being able to hear would be scary for me. My room has a door in the corner and its own sink straight ahead. The window is opposite the door, and my bed is to the right of the door.

#everydayrainbows: it's nice of the nurses to give me my own room

Daring to hope

Someone called an audiologist – Martin – came to see me today. Professor Ramsden did put the foreign body in my head in the end. I decided I might as well give it a go. Mum really wanted me to have it and she said if I really didn't like it, I didn't have to wear it. She said there was nothing to lose by trying it. In a few weeks, Martin will switch it on so we know if it works (it won't, I know). Martin said the operation went well. I don't know how he knows that, and it's weird being told the operation that took away my hearing went well. Massive #everydayrainbows, though: I understood Martin just fine! I could lipread him. I actually felt like I had a normal conversation with someone. Well, normal if talking about foreign bodies in heads is normal. But he spoke to me. Actually to me, not to someone else about me. When he left, I felt a tiny bit of hope that things might be OK.

I squashed it quickly. I don't dare hope because I always end up disappointed, but there was a tiny bit of hope there before I squashed it.

Moving

Tomorrow I have to move out of my room onto the main ward, where lots of other patients are. It's to get me used to being with people before I go home.

Giant

Being on the main ward is like watching a silent movie all the time, and I can't turn the movie off. I can see people talking but I can't hear them. I can see machines flashing, and I know they beep because I remember, but I can't hear anything. Sometimes I lie here and beg my ears to work. Who would have thought I'd ever talk to my ears? I tell them sound is there for them to hear, and I tell them to remember that they know how to hear. But *nothing at all*.

This morning a doctor I've not seen before came to see me before Mum arrived to visit, so I was on my own. The doctor was very tall, and seemed even taller from where I was lying in my bed. He looked like a giant.

He stood at the end of my bed and started talking. I tried hard to read his lips, but I couldn't. He was talking really fast, so I told him, 'I can't hear.' (I still find it really hard to say the d word – 'deaf'.) He leaned over, put his face really close to mine, and started shouting. I could tell he was shouting. Even shouting didn't get through. Nothing can get into my silence. I just said, 'Yes.' Anything to make him go away.

Deaf and blind

I can only write in the daytime now. At night-time, my eyes have to be taped shut because I got an infection in them. I thought not being able to hear was scary, but not being able to hear *or* see is worse.

When I was at junior school, we would ask each other if we would rather be deaf or blind. What would you say? Most people said they'd rather be deaf. I said I'd rather be blind. And I'm the one who ends up not being able to hear.

But we never thought about what it would be like to be deaf *and* blind. Now I know. It's terrifying.

Last night when the nurse came to tape my eyes shut, she stopped, and then she wrote me a note: 'It must be scary?' I nodded. Then she wrote some more: 'If you need anything in the night, press your buzzer, and I will come. I will put your finger on my ring, so you know it's me helping you.' That made me feel a bit better. Even when I can't see or hear her, at least I'll know who is there.

#everydayrainbows: that nurse

Wheelchair

I've got to go in a wheelchair today to see an eye doctor. It's
in a different part of the hospital and I can't walk far yet. I'm
working on my walking, though, so hopefully I will soon be
able to walk.

Eye doctor

The eye doctor was in a different building completely, so
I had to go outside to get there. I've still got the massive
bandage on my head that they put there after my operation.
When I was outside, there were loads of people around,
walking to different places, and it feels as if I'm not one
of them now. I'd forgotten that some people have normal
lives that don't involve hospitals and brain tumours and
wheelchairs and ears that don't hear. It still feels as if I'm in a
bubble. Maybe I'll get out of the bubble soon?

The eye doctor's waiting room was really busy. People were
sitting on all the chairs. I couldn't see the chairs because they
all had people sitting on them, but I bet they were blue.
Mum parked my wheelchair by a wall, and we waited. Mum
had to stand because there were no chairs and I felt bad that
she had to stand. My head hurt; this was the first time since
surgery it had been off my pillow for so long, and I think
my neck had forgotten how to hold it up. After ages, the

doctor called my name. Well, I assume he did. I didn't hear him, but Mum pushed my chair to his room, so he must have called me.

The doctor said he was going to sew one of my eyes closed, to help it heal. I couldn't understand him, but Mum told me. And Mum told the doctor, 'No.' She never says no to doctors! I don't know why she did this time, but I'm glad she took control, because I can't really concentrate or think at the moment, but I know I don't want my eye sewing shut.

I'm glad to be back in bed. Soon be time for my eyes to be taped shut, though.

Silent journey

Now that I refused the eye treatment, there is no reason for me to stay in hospital, so they're sending me home.

Mum helped me pack my bag while Dad got the car. I thought maybe it was only in the hospital I can't hear, but it's not. I can't hear in the car. No Classic FM. Mum and Dad haven't got the radio on, I can see that.

It's a silent journey home.

Not brave

Kirsty, Pollyanna and Aunty Jane were waiting when we got home. It was horrid not being able to hear them. I walked past the piano. Well, limped; my walking is still not great. I wasn't brave enough to play a note on the piano, because I didn't want to not hear it.

#everydayrainbows: my sisters

Under my bed

My flute is in my bedroom, in its case, under my bed. Before, it was out all the time. Now I don't even try to play it. I did when it was just my face that was the problem, but now it's my hearing as well. I still need my flute with me, though. That's why it's under my bed.

Scary

I'm eating lots of Chocolate Buttons. It's scary being home and not being able to hear.

#everyday rainbows: Chocolate Buttons

I know

I know that my redeemer
liveth . . .

Friends?

I had a text from Jodie today.
She wants to come and see
me. I want to see her, but I'm
scared to. What if we can't be
friends, now I can't hear? We've been friends since we were 5,
but never when one of us can't hear the other. I don't want to
not be friends. I texted back: 'not today'.

Text

Jodie keeps texting. I can't keep saying no, can I? So she's
coming this afternoon. I hope it goes OK.

All good

It was fine! I can lipread Jodie and we just chatted like we
normally do. Loads of things are changing for me but I'm glad
Jodie is not one of them.

#everydayrainbows: Jodie

Christmas

It's nearly Christmas. I did all my Christmas shopping
before my operation. Hard to believe I was so organized!
But Christmas is a rubbish time not to be able to hear. Well,
all time is, really, but especially Christmas. There's all the
Christmas music and concerts, for a start. I have to miss them.
And then there's things like games. Do you know how many
games there are where you need to hear? Even 'Charades'.
I know that's miming/acting, but you need to hear people
calling out the guesses. I'm not looking forward to Christmas.

#everydayrainbows: I don't need to shop

Game

Aunty Jane sorted a game so I could play it! It must have
taken her ages, but she wrote everything down so I could
follow. It was a sort of quiz game.

#everydayrainbows: Aunty Jane

2001

Why me?

I used to like New Year. I was 12
when I first stayed up and saw the

New Year in; my friend was sleeping over and we both stayed awake till midnight. I stopped liking New Year when I was 18. That's when I realized that things I wanted for my life, like university and being a teacher, were not going to happen because of NF2.

At New Year, everyone says, 'What was good about last year?', 'What are you hoping for this year?', 'What's your New Year's resolution?' and stuff. I never used to even think to hope a New Year wouldn't include hospitals, but now it doesn't occur to me to hope it won't. Hospitals are part of my life now. What's exciting about a New Year of hospitals and operations? Nothing.

Jeremiah 29:11 in the Bible says: '"I know what I have planned for you," says the Lord. "I have good plans for you. I don't plan to hurt you. I plan to give you hope and a good future."'

I know God knows his plans for my life, and that they are good. Somehow. Even if I can't see it. It doesn't mean I have to like his plans, though, does it? How come he has nice plans for everyone else but not me? I know he loves me just as much as them, he loves everyone the same, but it's really hard to see everyone else doing things I'll never be able to do now, and all because of stupid NF2. Even so, I do trust God. Life is hard enough anyway, without turning my back on him and making it worse.

When I was little, I learned that FAITH means Forsaking All I Trust Him. Him is God. It means that whatever happens, and when I don't understand, if I have faith, nothing stops me trusting God.

135

When I was feeling really fed up and sad a while ago, I thought, 'Why me?' then I thought, 'Why not me?' At least if I have NF2, it means someone else doesn't have to have it. That doesn't make sense, does it? But it's what I thought.

I still don't like New Year, though.

#everydayrainbows: faith

Morse Code

I thought being deaf was the worst thing that could happen. Then I thought the foreign body not working was the worst thing that could happen. Now I think the worst thing is if the foreign body *does* work. Well, I don't think it, I know it. Today, I sat in a little room with a computer in one corner. Martin was there and he attached wires, going from the computer to my head, before 'switch-on' as he called it. That means before turning the wires on and seeing if the foreign body (or ABI, to call it by its real name) works. Just before switch-on, people crowded into the room because they all wanted to know if it worked. I felt like I was in a zoo, sitting in front of a crowd of people all watching me. I also saw a machine which would get my heart going if one of the wires gave me a heart attack. I tried to ignore that machine. Martin pressed buttons on the computer, and eventually I heard a noise. It was the most horrid, screechy-buzzy-beepy noise. It kind of made me shiver, like when people used to run their nails down the chalkboard at school. So I didn't tell anyone, because I didn't think that could be the noise they wanted

136

me to hear. Martin kept pressing buttons, and the chalkboard screechy noise kept coming. In the end, I said I'd heard something. All the crowd started clapping and cheering, but I didn't. This is it? It's not like hearing, but 'heard' is the only word I can use to describe it. It's a bit like Morse Code. Beep beep. But I never learned Morse Code. Beep beep beep.

Operation

I knew it. I knew this year would mean more operations. It's April now, and guess what? I need an operation. Not on my brain this time, on my leg. Oh yes, the tumours can grow anywhere, and this one decided to grow on my leg. Mr Taylor says it'll just be a little operation and I don't even need to stay in hospital overnight, so at least that's something. Even after all this time, I don't like staying in hospital. Practise does not make perfect.

#everydayrainbows: it's not a big
operation

Children

I went to Discoverers at church today for the first time since I went deaf. Not to help, but just to see the children. It was nice to see them, but I was sad that I couldn't really understand what they said. I think I'd thought I still would be able to. I hoped I would be able to, anyway.

Identity

I saw Dr Margaret last week. I'm glad she knows sign language and what it's like not to hear. We talked about my identity as a deaf person. She asked what my hobbies are, and I realized I would still say hearing things like theatre and cinema and music. Nothing has replaced those hobbies, so what makes me *me* now? Why am I here? What's the point? I can't do the things that used to make me me any more. I still feel like a hearing person, but I'm not a hearing person! I wish I knew what God has in store for me. If he has anything in store. Or will I just exist like this for the next fifty years? Why?

Conversation with God

The operation on my leg went fine. I'm home. I have a bandage on my leg, but I can walk. It's strange being able to walk after an operation when I normally can't. I need to tell you about what happened, though; I think it might be important.

It was the usual start to an operation. Hospital gown, lie on the bed, get wheeled down long corridors to theatre. It was the long corridor that did it. As I lay there, something inside me sort of snapped. Do you know what I mean? It was like I stepped back and looked at my life, but I wasn't looking at my life. Not really. I was looking at someone else's. My life is

138

not supposed to involve hospitals and operations. It would be better if I had no life. I told God not to let me wake up after the anaesthetic. It would be best if I just died. I'm going to write the rest as a conversation between me and God, because that's what it was.

Me: Don't let me wake up.
God: You'll wake up.
Me: But how am I supposed to live this life I don't want?
God: You need to let go.
Me: I know! That's why I want to die.
God: You don't need to let go of life. You need to let go of what you thought life would be.

So that's what I think might be important.

It's funny, though: I always worry that I won't wake up after anaesthetic, and then the one time I don't want to wake up, I worried that I would wake up.

I really hate anaesthetic.

#everydayrainbows: God is with me

How?

I need to let go of what I thought life would be? How am I supposed to do that?

Scar

I got the stitches out of my leg. The scar is S-shaped. I don't know why, none of my others are. I've had so many operations, I think I've got more scar than skin!

#everydayrainbows: my leg is healing really well

Never

Mum keeps asking when I'm going to get rid of my flute. Um, never? I think God is asking me, too, but every time he does, I quickly ignore it. My flute is staying with me.

Still never

God keeps asking. It's getting hard to ignore him.

Never never never

Flute is still under my bed. I don't dare open the case. I don't want to see all I've lost. Because I have lost it, haven't I? I don't think I'm ever going to get better. NF2 is here to stay. There's no light at the end of the tunnel. I wish there was.

I know

I know that my redeemer
liveth . . .

Sophie

Sophie is back from Zambia.
It's hard, not hearing her, and
I was really nervous about
seeing her. She was nervous,
too. I think we'll be OK. I hope we will. We just need to learn
how to get past my silence. It's really nice to see her, though:
#everydayrainbows

Missing pages

I don't feel like a deaf person. I'm a hearing person who can't
hear. It's hard to understand what people are saying, and
everyone's lips move differently when they talk. The hearing
therapist told me that only 35 per cent of words are visible on
the lips anyway. That's like trying to read a book with more
than half the pages missing. Can you imagine doing that?
Every time I talk to someone, I'm trying to read a book with
most of the pages missing. People say I'm good at it, but I
don't think I am, and it's hard work. I have to concentrate a
lot, and it's really tiring. If there's lots of people, it's worse.

At dinner, there are six of us. Mum, Dad, my three sisters and me, all around the table. Everyone talks, sometimes more than one person at a time. It's hard to lipread them. My sisters talk about their days at school and college, and all they've been doing. I don't have anything to say; I just try to get through my days. But it's hard when the others are talking about all the things I can't do any more. Anyway, even if I had something to say – which I don't – I wouldn't know when to say it. I never used to think about it, conversation was so easy, but now I don't know when to speak, and every time I try, I feel like I'm interrupting someone. It's easier if I just eat my dinner and don't say anything.

Deaf Club

I've decided to go to the Deaf Club. I'll fit in better there, where no one can hear.

'You're not deaf'

The Deaf Club was a nightmare. I was nervous when I walked in, but I made myself do it. A lady came over, and I said, 'Hello, my name is Emily.' I did it in sign language as I said it. I'm still not great at sign language, but I can say my name. The lady said, in sign language, 'You're not deaf.' I felt like I'd been punched.

I just nodded. I am. She said, 'No you're not, you can talk.' So I had to try to convince her that I can't hear. Like I need reminding. She didn't believe me. I'm never going back there. Now I know what Sally meant when she said there is 'Deaf' which means people who are born deaf and can't really talk, and there is 'deafened' which means people who have lost their hearing and can talk. Now I know that Deaf people don't think deaf people are deaf. Does that make sense to you? I don't think it does to me!

2003

Maybe

God is still reminding me about my flute. Maybe I should think about getting rid of it. Maybe.

Definitely maybe

I should think about getting rid of it. I know I should. I don't want to.

ABI rainbow - at last

I remembered I need to update you on my implant. Remember how much I hated it when it was first switched on? Well, that was two years ago, and I hated it for a long time. I hoped it would make me hear, but it doesn't. I still have the buzz-beep noise, but slowly, slowly, slowly, I

143

am learning. I have to pair up the buzz-beep with the shape I see on someone's lips and, when I manage it, it helps me with lipreading. I don't always manage it, but I do quite a lot. Isn't that great? I'm glad Mum told me to have the implant. I'm still sad it doesn't make me hear, though. I tried 'listening' to music with it, and it sounded like a cat screeching. I couldn't stand it; I had to stop the music.

#everydayrainbows: I am learning

My flute

I've just put my flute back in its case. For the first time since I lost my hearing, I put the case on my bed, sat down next to it, and opened it. There was my flute, all three pieces of it, lying on red velvet. After a long time, I put the three pieces together and held the flute in my hands. This is what I used to play. This is what I used to love. I lifted my flute to my lips and played a note. It made a horrid noise in my ABI. Maybe if I took the hearing aid bit of my ABI off, I would be able to hear when I played the flute? I tried it, but my silence didn't change. The note didn't get through. I didn't even 'hear' through the vibrations, like Clare's cousin said I might. I should have known I wouldn't. I tried again. Nothing.

I held the flute for a long time. Then, for the last time, I took it apart and rested it in its red velvet casing. 'OK,' I said to God and to myself. 'I'm ready to let go.'

I'm determined to find a rainbow today.

#everydayrainbows: my flute is beautiful

Jehovah-jireh

Today I gave my flute away. It was only yesterday I told God I was ready to let go, but I didn't really mean this soon! A friend came round and God told me to give her my flute. I know she plays the flute, but I wasn't sure why she needs mine as well as hers. I asked her if she wanted mine, and she couldn't believe it. Apparently she hasn't got a flute, but really wants one, and has been praying for one. Her husband even told her God would provide her with a flute.

Jehovah-jireh is one of God's names. You can read about it in Genesis 22. Jehovah-jireh means 'God will provide'. God provided my friend with a flute because I let go, just like he told me to in that corridor on the way to theatre. In my head I am glad she has the flute. I'm glad in most of my heart too, but I still wish I could play it. I'm happy God provided for her. Will he provide for me, as well?

Maybe one day I won't feel so sad that it's not me playing my flute.

#everydayrainbows: my flute is making music

What's most important?

Philippians 1:21 says, 'To me the only important thing about living is Christ.'

A few months before I lost my hearing, I went to a wedding, and one of the songs was about this verse. It really made me think. It means the most important thing in life is living for Jesus. I know Jesus is the reason I'm alive – it's a miracle that I haven't died by now. But what if I start really saying 'living is Christ'? Is Jesus the most important thing in my life?

2004

Bridesmaid

Jodie's getting married, and she asked me to be her bridesmaid. Even though I can't hear, and I have a wonky face, she still asked me. I feel bad that I will spoil the day. Everyone will look at me, and I will ruin the photos with my wonky face. But Jodie wants me anyway, and she's my best friend. We always said that we'd be each other's bridesmaid. I don't think I'll ever get married, but I'm happy Jodie is. And Adam is really nice. When I met him, I thought, 'Yeah, he's good enough for her!' We went dress shopping today. The wedding's not for a few months, but we wanted to get the dress in the sales if we could. I got a gold, strapless dress. It's gorgeous! I'm glad Jodie doesn't want me to wear something

I don't like. My shoes are flat, though. I wish I could wear heels. People say I'm tall enough without them, but I still wish I could wear them. Stupid bad balance.

#everydayrainbows: Jodie wants me

Tomorrow!

#everydayrainbows: it's Jodie's wedding tomorrow

Dress falls down

I went to Jodie's house to get ready for the wedding. Jodie has been looking after my dress since we bought it; I put it on and did the zip up at the back, but when I let go, the dress fell down. I mean literally fell down. My dress wouldn't stay up! No straps to hold it up, and I forgot about that. I've lost some weight recently and, if I'd thought about it, I'd have tried the dress on again before today, but I didn't think about it. It's not as though I've been trying to lose weight. The wedding is in two hours. Jodie's mum pinned my dress to my bra to hold the dress up, and I will keep my stole wrapped around me at all times!

#everydayrainbows: safety pins

Wedding

It was hard not being able to hear at the wedding. I sometimes wish I could have my hearing back just for a day, but I know a day wouldn't be enough. When we sang the songs at the wedding, I did sign language. Well, I was going to, but I felt a bit embarrassed to do it when I was sitting at the front. Normally I prefer to sit at the back of things. One of the songs was 'All Things Bright and Beautiful'. I know I'm not beautiful, but I wish I was normal again. I wish I didn't limp when I walked. I don't even know why I've started limping more, but I have. So I limped down the aisle as well as wobbled. Even in flat shoes, my balance is still rubbish. At least I didn't drop my flowers! The song talks about God making everything. I still try not to think about Psalm 139. So in the songs, I just sang them in my head. I can still remember the music, as long as I have heard it before. 'All Things Bright and Beautiful'. Jodie looked so beautiful today. I sang that song in my head for her.

#everydayrainbows: I can still hear music in my head

I've shrunk!

I had my annual health check at my GP today. Things like height and weight and just checking I'm OK. The weird thing today was that I am half an inch smaller than I used to be. I've been 5ft 10 for ages but this time I was 5ft 9½. The doctor didn't seem bothered, though.

Laughing

Professor Ramsden wants to do a surgery on me called a nerve graft, which might help my face not be so wonky. The thing is, I don't have to have it. It should be easy to go ahead, though, shouldn't it? You know how much I hate my face. But it's really hard to have a surgery that I don't have to have, if you see what I mean. It was funny when Professor Ramsden told me about the operation; he wanted to show me a clip of what someone looked like before and after surgery, but he couldn't work the TV. This is the man who operates on my brain!

#everydayrainbows: laughing, even in hospital

Sore back

Every year I have to have a scan of my brain to check if there are tumours. Last time, the surgeon told me there are but they are small enough that we can just leave them at the moment. So, right now, I have tumours in my brain. That has become such a normal thing. I told the surgeon (Mr Waters) that my back is sore. Not my whole back, just one area low down. He said OK, but wasn't worried.

#everydayrainbows: my brain tumours have not grown big

Wait and see

I had the nerve graft surgery on my face; I decided to go ahead in the end, but I wasn't sure for ages. I actually only decided as I was in the car on the way to see Professor Ramsden! It just felt right to say yes. Now I have to wait and see if it worked. Professor Ramsden says the nerves will take months to start working together (if they work together at all).

2006

Not worried

I had my yearly scan again. Hard to believe a whole year has gone by since my last one. Brain tumours have grown a bit but still don't need anything doing. I told Mr Waters my back is still sore. He wasn't worried.

#everydayrainbows: I don't need brain surgery

Too big

I'm going to be a bridesmaid again! I was so surprised when Louise asked me. I'd never have thought she would. Today I tried on my bridesmaid's dress, which is a long skirt and a separate bodice. The bodice bit fitted fine, but the skirt was too big. I've gone so skinny, I expect I've got a tumour growing somewhere. Remember the doctors said the tumours would grow on my nerves wherever they liked? Well, they do. Tumours pop up all over. Do you think it's weird that I talk about tumours as though they are normal? One thing I've learned about tumours is that they can make me lose weight. I'd never have thought they'd do that; they do it even before an operation. It's like, as they grow inside me, they suck me in, and they get bigger and I get smaller.

#everydayrainbows: the shop is going to make my skirt smaller so it fits

2007–08

Bought cakes

Yearly scan again. I told Mr Waters my back is still sore. I told him that when I am in the car and it goes over a speed bump, I have to lift myself off the seat because the bump makes my lower back feel like it's on fire. Lots of things make it feel like that now. Like fire, or like I'm being stabbed. Even turning round, or going up a step makes it stab. But I've got a high pain threshold and usually try to ignore the fire. I only told Mr Waters about it because Mum said I should. I don't know why that would make a difference; I've already told him it really hurts. But when I told him about the speed bumps, he looked worried. Then he took me out of his office and down a corridor to where there was a hospital bed. He told me to lie flat on my back and keep my legs straight. Then he lifted my foot up. When it was only about 5cm from the bed, I screamed. I mean, really screamed! I'm surprised the whole hospital didn't hear. It was so painful. Mr Waters put my foot back on the bed and then we walked back to his office.

I could tell something was really wrong. Mr Waters said, 'You have a tumour in your spine. We need to operate, and when you wake up, you might be paralysed from the waist down.' Paralysed? What! That means I won't be able to move my legs, doesn't it? How will I get around? How will I get dressed? There's no way I can put my socks on if I can't bend my knees. Stupid 'Mummy Longlegs'. Stupid NF2. This tumour must be why my clothes are too big. I walked out of Mr Waters' room in shock. Well, I limped. Maybe soon I won't even be able to limp. I went to the hospital coffee shop with Mum and Dad where we bought drinks and sat at one of the tables. There was nothing to say. Dad looked like he was going to be sick.

Mum bought cakes. She never buys cakes unless she's had bad news. I make her buy lots of cakes. I feel bad about that.

Louise

I went straight to church from the hospital, because it was Louise's wedding rehearsal. I practised walking down the aisle behind Louise, and afterwards she gave me a hug.

#everydayrainbows: Louise

152

Ugly

Today was Louise's wedding. It was a beautiful day, the sun was shining, and I managed to walk down the aisle after Louise. I didn't know if I would, because my walking is really bad now, it's like I have to sort of roll my right hip and leg over every time I take a step. That doesn't really make sense, but it's how it feels. Normally, legs just swing forward to take a step, but mine rolls over into the step. I'm glad I made it down the aisle. I would have been so embarrassed if I'd fallen flat on my face in front of everyone there. Flat on my wonky face. After the service, it was time for photos. I still don't like having my photo taken, but I knew I could do it, because I did it at Jodie's wedding. Mum says I'm beautiful, but she's got to say that, hasn't she, because she's my mum? I know I'm not beautiful.

#everydayrainbows: I didn't fall over

2009

New Year

New Year again and, as we know by now, it never brings good news. I'm having more trouble than usual eating. Chewing has been hard since my face got damaged, but now it's hard to swallow things. It's like I have something in my throat getting in the way. The doctors want to do some tests, so I've got to go and stay in hospital while I have them. What a way to start the New Year. Can you see why I don't like New Year?

Watching lips

It's a bit boring being in hospital. OK, very boring. It's not like I've had an operation or anything. I've been thinking about what I wrote before about Jodie. We've always been friends. Like, always. Ever since we first met when we were 5. Even when I sort of pushed her away that time when I went deaf. I only did that because I was scared. Jodie is really the only friend I have of my age who knew me before I was deaf, but I think that's OK. People ask me if other friends left me when I was having a hard time, but they didn't, they just went off to university and things. Anyway, I like that most of my friends now have only known me since I was deaf, because it's just normal for them. Apart from me lipreading them! But they are all great and don't seem to mind me watching their lips. I think they are better than I would be if someone watched my lips.

#everydayrainbows: people who let me lipread them

Bad news

It's strange being in hospital but not having an operation or feeling really ill. I have lost some more weight because it's hard to swallow food, but I'm OK. It reminds me of that first time, when I was not feeling ill and the nurses let me have the day room. This time I am allowed out in-between tests; I had a scan, then I went to the hospital shop to buy chocolate (I can eat chocolate!). When I got back, there was a crowd around the nurses' desk. I went to walk past, and one of my surgeons stepped forward. He had my scan pictures in his hand, but his face told me it was bad news. I have two tumours in my throat. There is a millimetre gap between them. That's tiny, isn't it? If they grow any more, that's it. My airway will be blocked. I won't be able to breathe. I managed to have a conversation about it – I need to see another doctor tomorrow – and then I went to my hospital room and cried.

#everydayrainbows: chocolate

Honest

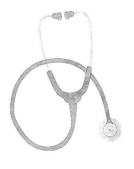

I saw the new doctor this morning, Mr Barry. He's an ear, nose and throat surgeon. He looked at my scans, then said the tumours would have to come out. I asked him if he had ever done this sort of surgery before, and he said, 'No.' That actually made me feel more confident about him! He's honest with me. He said he will only operate if he can be sure there is an intensive care bed available for me to go to, because he thinks surgery might make me end up in intensive care. Again. And he wants me to stay in hospital until he gets a theatre slot to operate. Who knows how long that will be? But I think he's really worried my airway will stop letting air through.

Shopping

After I'd seen Mr Barry, Mum and I went out of the hospital
for a bit. I'm allowed to do that, as long as I tell the nurses
I'm going and when I'll be back. Mum had been staying at a
hotel near the hospital, but two nights ago the nurse in charge
here said she could sleep in my room. My room is massive,
and there's a spare bed in it anyway, but it's really nice of that
nurse. I feel bad when Mum has to pay for a hotel because of
me. So we went out. We felt like we were skipping school or
something! We went to this big shopping centre and bought
me some new trousers. That was Mum's idea. It turns out
I'm a size smaller now. I know my clothes feel a bit big, but
I didn't know I was a whole size smaller. I wonder if Mum
guessed, though. Maybe this not being able to eat thing is
worse than I thought. The trousers will look good with my
boots, hopefully.

Pizza

We had dinner out as well, and I
managed to eat it. Italian, because
that's my favourite now. It's my
favourite because it's the easiest to eat. I used to choose food I
liked; now I choose what I can actually eat.

#everydayrainbows: my mum

Surprise!

Surgery went well! I can't even see the scars, because Mr Barry went through my mouth to reach my throat. Surgery was yesterday, and I can go home today. My throat feels sore, but ice cream helps! Mr Barry came to see me on the ward to tell me all had gone well. And he had a surprise for me. Before surgery, I'd asked him if I could see one of the tumours afterwards. I mean, I've had so many tumours removed, and I've never even seen one. Mr Barry said no, because the tumour had to go to be tested (that's called 'histology' or something) once it's been removed. The surprise was when he got his phone out to show me photos of the tumour he'd taken for me! I didn't think the tumour would have red on it. I thought it would be white, like tumours look on scans, but blood makes sense, since it was inside me.

It looked a bit like a ball. Mr Barry said it was like a golf ball! No wonder swallowing was hard.

#everydayrainbows: Mr Barry taking that photo for me

Golf balls gone

It's nice not having golf balls in my throat!

#everydayrainbows: swallowing isn't so hard

Praying

I wonder if I will ever get a break from hospitals? It's back
surgery this time. The time has come for the operation
Mr Waters said might mean I can't walk any more. I'm praying
I won't be paralysed. The surgery is soon, and I'm scared.

Walking

I'm in hospital in
Manchester. Tomorrow I
have the surgery on my
back. I have prayed so
much that I will be able
to walk after the surgery. I
walked into hospital. I hope
I walk out.

Bossy

Mum and Dad and I went out for dinner, like we normally do
before I have surgery. It's really nice of them to take me out.
It gets me away from the hospital and away from the hospital
food! We never used to eat out. Well, not often, and when we
did it was because my grandparents took us. Eating out was
a treat, something special. It still feels like that, even though
I know I'm having an operation tomorrow, which is not a
treat at all. I'm quite bossy with my brain and stop it thinking

about the bad stuff too much. I have to, otherwise I'd just think about NF2 all the time.

#everydayrainbows: good memories

Working together

I can remember waking up after surgery. I tried to move my legs, but they wouldn't move. They were really painful, though. Mum told me that all Mr Waters had said was 'Sorry'. I feel bad that he said sorry. He did his best, didn't he? When he opened up my back to see my spine, he thought he couldn't operate, because it was too difficult to get to the tumour. In the end, he asked someone to come and help, and they worked it out together. I'll tell you what they did. They actually moved my spine, took the tumours out – oh yes, there were two – and then put my spine back! Mr Waters said he didn't know how I'd managed with so much pain for so long. I feel really bad that he said sorry. I don't blame him that my legs are paralysed and don't move, but I didn't think it would actually happen.

#everydayrainbows: Mr Waters

Paralysed

I've been in hospital for three weeks now. Just lying in bed, or propped up in bed with pillows. The physios come to see if my legs are still paralysed. They always are. They are just two long bumps under the blanket that never move but hurt all the time – especially if someone bumps into my bed as they walk past. Tomorrow is my birthday. Another birthday in hospital. Happy birthday to me.

Birthday cake

The nurses organized a cake for me! Everyone on the ward sang 'Happy Birthday' and shared the cake. I don't like my birthday, because it just reminds me that I nearly died and of how much my life has changed. My life does have good things in it (#everydayrainbows!) but it's not a life to celebrate. And I've had lots of birthdays in hospital or recovering from hospital or waiting to go into hospital. Birthdays have always been a big thing in my family, and I feel like I'm letting everyone down, so I try to pretend I'm happy. Secret: I'm not happy, though.

#everydayrainbows: people being nice

Pray out loud

Andrew came to visit today! He drove for more than two and a half hours, just to visit me. I met Andrew before I knew anything about NF2; he was the leader of my first-ever beach mission team. There were about twenty-five of us on the team, and the first night, we had a meeting to plan the week. At the end, Andrew said, 'Right, we are going to go round the circle, and everyone is going to pray out loud.' I couldn't believe it. People would probably think I'd be fine with praying out loud, given my church background, but actually I'm really shy about it. If he'd said 'read aloud from the Bible' then OK. But he didn't say that. Can you imagine how nervous I was? I was sitting about halfway round the group, and so while the first half took it in turns to pray, I rehearsed in my head what I was going to say. When it came to my turn, I recited it. Beach mission had a few firsts (remember the accordion I had to quickly learn to play?).

Boring

Another first was to give my testimony. That means tell my story about my life. And not just tell my story, but tell it while I was standing on a box on the seafront, with people walking past. How scary. As the week went on, other people did it, but not me, and I thought maybe I wouldn't have to. But on the very last night, Andrew made me stand on the box and talk.

I remember thinking my story is really boring. 'Born into a Christian family, became a Christian when I was 5.' Other people talk about big things happening, like never knowing God and suddenly realizing he's there, or doing really naughty things and being miraculously saved from them. Back then I wished I had a big thing in my life. I have a big thing now, and I wish I didn't, and now I know I was wrong, and it wasn't a boring story before.

Funeral

Anyway, Andrew came to visit. He's great, despite making me do those things before! Back when everyone thought I would die, Sophie planned my funeral, and she decided that Andrew would take the service. I think that was a good choice. I would have chosen him as well.

Sophie planned it all. She even decided I would be buried in the red dress I wore when we had the family photo taken when we didn't know if I would die.

When Andrew visited, we hardly talked about hospital stuff at all. We talked about the Bible and other books, and Andrew really listened to things I said. For the time he was visiting, I felt normal. I forgot I was in a hospital bed and my legs don't move any more.

#everydayrainbows: Andrew

Twitch

My leg moved! My left leg. Just a twitch, but it definitely moved! I thought someone had walked past my bed – it always hurts if they brush past my blankets – but *no one had walked past.* Does this mean I'm not paralysed?

#everydayrainbows: moving blankets

Half a centimetre

Mr Waters said it doesn't mean I will definitely walk again, but it means there's a chance. The physio came to see me and when she pulled the blankets back, I saw my matchstick legs stretching down the bed. She asked me to move my leg. I tried really hard, but I couldn't do it.

After the physio left, I tried and tried to get my leg to move. I begged it to. 'Please move, leg. Please.' In the end, it moved about half a centimetre along the bed. Only half a centimetre! That's tiny, isn't it?

Later, I tried it again. And the next day. When the physio came, I showed her. Half a centimetre is a start.

#everydayrainbows: half a centimetre

Not an emergency

They're sending me to a hospital nearer home. I still can't walk, or even sit up for very long, so I have got to go home in an ambulance. I can lie down in that. They keep saying it'll be today, but it never is. They have to wait till an ambulance is available; I'm not an emergency so I can wait.

Blue lights

I'm in Leicester hospital now. I had to leave Manchester in a rush because suddenly an ambulance was available. Mum quickly put all my stuff in a bag, then went to her hotel to pack her own.

While she was gone, people came to take me to the ambulance. A special NF2 nurse had just come to visit me as well, so she walked to the ambulance beside my bed as it was pushed along.

Mum arrived, threw her bags into the ambulance, climbed in herself and then we left. I didn't really have time to say goodbye to people on the ward. I'm sad about that but it's OK because I don't like goodbyes. I asked the ambulance driver to put the blue lights on, but he said they are for emergency only. At least I'm not an emergency. But when I looked at the red blanket over my legs in the ambulance, having legs that don't work felt like an emergency to me. It is an emergency, isn't it?

In Manchester, I was in a hospital bay on the ward with two other people, so there were only three of us. In Leicester, I'm on a ward with about twenty people. My bed is the nearest to the door, so there are always people coming and going. I feel like I'm in a goldfish bowl: I can't get away from people watching me. If I could walk away, I would. Or even just walk to close the curtains around my bed. But I'm stuck. I wish my legs worked.

#everydayrainbows: the ambulance

Waving

Every day, I lie here in bed. If I could hear, it might not be quite so bad, but I can see all the other patients lying in their beds, talking across the ward to each other, and I can't join in. They're too far away for me to lipread.

There's one patient who is about three beds down from me on the opposite side who looks really nice. Sometimes she waves to me. My mum must have told her I'm deaf. Mum always talks to all the other patients; they love her!

I'm glad I've got you to talk to.

#everydayrainbows: my diary

But God
is my
STRENGTH
HE IS MINE
forever!

Standing

The physio came today to have a look at me. Now, if I have help, I can move from my bed to sitting in a chair, and the physio wondered if I can stand. She said she wanted me to stand still for a whole minute, without holding on to anything. I was determined to do it, so she helped me to stand, then let go of me. I stared at a square on the curtain really hard. I know doing that helps me balance. I stood for a whole minute! It was exhausting, but I did it. The physio said I should start using my ankles, not my eyes, to balance, but I can't remember what it's like to not have to balance with my eyes. I wonder if she knows about my brain tumours ruining my balance. Maybe I should tell her next time?

#everydayrainbows: one minute

She's a Christian!

The physio comes every day now and helps me stand. Today, I even walked! I took two steps! And the physio is a Christian. How great is that! #everydayrainbows!

I wouldn't want me

Sunday morning. 4 a.m. Yes, I'm awake. The sun woke me up, shining through a gap in the curtains, and I'm thinking about my church. It's weeks since I've been, and I really miss it. Maybe I can go today? I wish. Even if I was allowed out of the hospital, Mum says I'd never be able to climb into the car. I know she's right, really. If only my legs were better; two steps are not going to get me to church. Every time I look at my legs, I'm reminded of how useless I am. I can't even walk. God probably wouldn't want me at church anyway. Why would he? Even I wouldn't want me. I just make everything difficult. People have to speak clearly for me to lipread, and even then I don't always understand. I can't walk. All I can do is lie here.

No more goldfish bowl

We're moving wards in the hospital and the best thing is, I'm getting a room of my own! No more goldfish bowl. The nurse in charge came and asked me if I'd like a side room to myself on the new ward. I said, 'Only if no one else needs it,' and she said I could have it. She didn't say anything else, but I think she has guessed about the goldfish bowl.

#everydayrainbows: my own room

I can't go to the party

It's great having a room of my own, and it's more private when visitors come, too. When Sophie and Pollyanna visited today, it was just us and we could nearly pretend we weren't in a hospital. It's Mum's birthday soon, and we've been planning a party for ages, since before we even knew I'd need an operation on my back.

We didn't cancel our plans when I needed an operation, because I never thought the 'not walking thing' would happen to me. But it has. I can't walk. How am I going to get to a party?

I told Sophie and Pollyanna to go ahead with the party without me. I hate that NF2 ruins everything, and I'm not letting it ruin this.

My sisters sent me a text later: 'OK, we'll sort it.'

I know I'll have to try to be cheerful and not mind about missing out again. I've had lots of practise.

Cancelled

They've gone and cancelled the party! Now it's going to be just family, and it's going to be at the hospital. I can't leave, even for a day, so they are coming to me. We're going to have a picnic in the hospital grounds, and the nurses said I can go in my wheelchair. Another birthday in hospital. I feel bad for Mum. I've ruined something for her again.

Shuffling

The physio took me to the gym today. She parked my chair by two bars and asked me to stand up, hold on to them, and walk between them. Ha ha, what a joke. As if I can walk! We have been doing things to try to strengthen my legs, like lie on the bed and bend my knees, but I can't even do them very well. The bars helped, though, and I managed to shuffle along between them.

I always thought that if I walked again, it would feel great. It feels rubbish. So pathetic.

Church in hospital

Someone came to visit me today. He's a vicar and he works at the hospital. He's really kind, and he knows a bit of sign language. I was so surprised! He said if I want to go to the hospital church on Sunday, I can, and someone will take me in my wheelchair. I think I will go. Maybe Mum will come with me and do sign language for me, to tell me what's happening. Mum is really good at sign language now.

#everydayrainbows: sign language

Peace be with you

Church was amazing. It was in a room in the hospital, but the room really looked like a church. It had stained-glass windows and everything. At the end of the service, the vicar said, 'Peace be with you.' Then, because he saw I was there, he said, 'Peace be with you' in sign language. Then he saw someone else, who he must have visited too, and said 'Peace be with you' in Russian! I think it was Russian, anyway. Everyone was included.

Maybe God does still want me. I know in the Bible, in John 14:27, Jesus said, 'My peace I give you' and that his peace is not the same as people's peace. Maybe I really can have peace in this life I don't want to live. It's like that verse that said 'living is Christ'. Keep Jesus as the most important part of my life. I'm glad I went to church and God met me there.

#everydayrainbows: church

Uno!

Now I can walk a bit (with a Zimmer frame), I can go to the toilet without having to call for a nurse to help me get there! I'd never have thought I'd find that so exciting, but I do. That's how much my life has changed. Now it's not things like 'yippee, I won a race', it's 'yippee, I can walk to the toilet by myself'. I can also go out of my room if I want to.

In the ward opposite my room is the person I used to wave to on the other ward. I still wave to her when the physio takes me to the gym in my wheelchair, but today I thought I'd go and say hello properly, so I wobbled over to her on my Zimmer. When I got there, she had no choice but to meet me, because I collapsed in the chair by her bed! My legs wouldn't work any more; they needed to rest.

Her legs don't work either. Her name is Sheila, and it was great to talk to her. She's easy to lipread. We talked a lot about hospital, but we talked about other things too. It turns out Sheila is a Christian! So we talked about God as well. Sheila asked me if I wanted to go back over to her bed tomorrow and play 'Uno'. I don't know many card games but I do know 'Uno'! I never thought I'd say this about a day in hospital, but I'm quite looking forward to tomorrow.

Little-J is in my room with me, but it will be nice if I can have another friend here, too.

Lots of #everydayrainbows today!

Nicknames

Pollyanna sometimes calls me 'Emmy', which I like: she started it when she was little, so it's quite sweet.

One of my friends used to call me Twig because I'm tall and skinny. I know I didn't like being called 'Mummy Longlegs' at school, but Twig is OK. Maybe because I am older now. Or maybe because she called herself Blob. She's small, I'm tall. She's the one that made me the 'My mind and my body may become weak. But God is my strength. He is mine forever' cross stitch. To Twig, love from Blob.

Now I have another name: 'Uno Champ'. I've been going over to Sheila's bed every day, and we play lots of 'Uno'. She started calling me 'Uno Champ' because I keep winning! I don't normally win at 'Uno'.

#everydayrainbows: I'm glad I remembered about the nicknames and the cross stitch

Annoyed

Someone else has joined some of our 'Uno' games now, so there are three of us. Sheila gets really annoyed when people stand behind me and call my name when it's time for me to go to the gym.

She's not annoyed because our game stops, she's cross because they should know I can't hear them. She says to them, 'She's deaf, remember?' and that's how I know they are there. People are always forgetting I'm deaf, or forgetting to check I'm looking at them before they speak, so I'm used to it, but it's nice that Sheila sticks up for me.

#everydayrainbows: she never forgets

Feeling sad

It's Mum's 'party' tomorrow. Kirsty is in South Africa but everyone else is coming. Grandma, Grandad, Granny, Aunty

Jane, Sophie, Pollyanna and Mum and Dad. Mum doesn't know Aunty Jane is coming. It's a surprise, so Aunty Jane will come straight to the hospital from the train station, and hide in my room! Sophie will set up the tables and food outside and Pollyanna will come and help me get dressed. I used to dress her when she was a baby, and now she's dressing me. That makes me feel sad.

Then Pollyanna and Aunty Jane will push me in my wheelchair to meet the others, and we'll have the birthday picnic.

#everydayrainbows: my family

Funny!

The picnic was a bit of a disaster! It was fine at first, but then it got really windy and plates and food blew about. Then it started raining! So, where did my mum open her presents on her birthday? In a hospital canteen. Great. Not.

When I got back up to the ward, Sheila and some of the others started clapping! They'd seen us having our picnic – or not having it – out of the window, and thought it was really funny. I'm glad someone does! But it was quite funny: #everydayrainbows (in a weird sort of way!)

Chariots of Fire

I almost gave Sheila a heart attack today!
The physio gave me crutches to use instead
of a Zimmer frame. That means my walking
is getting a bit better. I'm not very good
with the crutches yet, though, and I wobble
all over the place. When Sheila saw me coming, she thought
I was going to fall over. She has decided they are going to
be called my chariots, and she will hum the *Chariots of Fire*
tune when she sees me coming, and pretend to conduct an
orchestra playing it. She's a bit crazy, and she makes me laugh!

I can remember the *Chariots of Fire* movie tune; it's some
of the music in my head. The movie is about Eric Liddell,
a great runner who ran for the glory of God. He said when
he ran, he made God happy because God made him good at
running so he was doing what God wanted. I can't run, but
I am learning to walk. Sort of. I feel bad for Sheila. She can't
walk at all.

Together

Sometimes Sheila and I pray together.

#everydayrainbows

174

Finally

Finally, I came home today. I didn't think I'd be away for so many weeks!

2010

Don't look at me

It's taken months and months but now I can walk with only one crutch. Indoors, I sometimes don't need one at all. I hold on to a chair or table or whatever is near me at the time. I've not thought of a song or a name for it! Maybe 'Furniture Walking'? I'd better text Sheila and ask for ideas.

What would you call it?

I still limp, and my balance is bad, but I can walk. My right leg is really, really skinny because the nerve that goes from my spine and down my right leg was damaged in the operation. I'm surprised the leg holds me up, but it does.

The doctor says the muscle might come back, but I don't think it will. Whenever they say a nerve might start working again, I get my hopes up, but it never happens. Like with my face. The doctor said then that the nerve wasn't actually cut, so my smile might come back. It didn't. Even after the nerve surgery on my face, my smile didn't come back. People say my face looks much better now, and it does look a bit less bad,

175

but it still feels bad to me. I'm really self-conscious about it. I hate it when people look at me.

#everydayrainbows: my face is less wonky now

Yes or no?

I'm giving my testimony at church on Sunday! Last week, I was asked if I would. I wanted to say no, but somehow I ended up saying yes.

Reasons for saying no:

- My memory is still bad so I won't remember what to say.
- I'm deaf so won't know how loudly I am talking, or if I am clear to hear or not. NB I never thought about that until I was deaf!
- Everyone will look at me and I hate it when people look at me.

Reasons for saying yes:

- I think it's what God wants me to do. I almost wish I didn't think that, but I do.

I also wish I had the 'boring' testimony I had when Andrew made me stand on that box and talk about my life. I was just a normal girl then. Now I don't think I'll ever feel normal again. So much has happened, my whole life has turned upside down. I probably couldn't even climb onto the box now, and even if I did, I'd overbalance and fall off.

God asks me to do hard things. They are *really* hard, but I do want to do what he wants. I wish it didn't hurt so much, though.

'Living is Christ.'

'No' reasons

Sunday is tomorrow. All my 'no' reasons are still there, big time.

Great Big Peace

It went OK! I sort of ignored the 'no' reasons. Well, I had to. The worst part was climbing up the two steps onto the platform in front of everyone. I still find steps really hard, and I was embarrassed to be struggling in front of them all.

I think speaking like that is what God wants me to do. As well as feeling nervous, I feel peace deep down inside me as well. There's a verse in the Bible, in Philippians 4:7, that talks about God's peace being something we can't understand, because it's too big. I think that's the peace I have about speaking. Speaking is scary, and what about my 'no' list? But I still feel a Great Big Peace, even though it doesn't make sense.

#everydayrainbows: Great Big Peace

Not happening

I've given my testimony at a few places now, and people keep saying I should write a book about my story, too. They've been saying that since I was first ill. I said no then, and I've said no every time ever since. I'm not writing a book. I love books, but I read them, I don't write them.

Fight

I've had another operation, this time on my eye, to try to help it close when I blink. It stopped blinking by itself after the operation that damaged my face. Now I'm lying in the middle bed on the left-hand side of the hospital ward, and I don't feel very close to God. I haven't for quite a long time. I know God's there and everything, but I used to feel closer to him. And now, as well as being deaf, with a wonky face and dodgy balance, I have a swollen eye. I look like I've been in a fight. I've never been in a real fight, though.

It closes!

I'm home now, and my eye is OK. It's not swollen any more, and it closes all by itself. I don't have to tape it shut every night.

#everydayrainbows: no tape

Nerve damage

There is a massive lump on my leg. At the back of my left thigh. I can actually see it. It hurts when I sit down.

This time I have to go to another hospital for the operation.

The doctor there said he can take the tumour away without damaging any nerves around it. Once, I'd have believed him, but now I know too much about nerve damage. There's always nerve damage. I hope he's right about me still being able to walk after the operation, though.

Red shoes

The operation was yesterday, and I came home today. I can still walk! Well, a bit, with two crutches. The doctor said not to try walking too much for now, so I've just typed 'shoes' online. I'm going to buy some new shoes! Maybe I was wrong about nerve damage never mending and stuff – I think this doctor has fixed my walking, so I want to buy a pair of shoes with heels for when I can walk. Last time I could walk in heels was when I was 13! I had some cream shoes I liked back then. This time I've chosen red ones, with a heel. I've ordered them and they should arrive next week. I can't wait to actually walk properly, after all this time. I hope my legs remember how!

#everydayrainbows: shoes

I can't

I'm so fed up. The shoes are a disaster.
I can't even stand in them before I lose
my balance. I should know by now
that I'm not normal. Normal people
can wear shoes like this. I can't. Mum is the same size feet as
me, so I've given the shoes to her. She says she'll wear them for
me, but I wish I could wear them myself. At least when I get to
heaven I can wear them. If anyone sees someone in red heels in
heaven, it'll be me!

It was Job, in the Bible, who said 'I know that my redeemer
liveth' like the last song I listened to before I went deaf. And
Job goes on to say he knows he will see God. He meant in
heaven. His life was really hard, but he still had hope. My life
is really hard, but I still have hope. God is with me, I know
that. And heaven is ahead.

#everydayrainbows: heaven

Hard work

I need another operation now. I'm not sure why I only seem to write in this diary when I need operations. Maybe it's because I always need operations! Or maybe it's because I can't talk to anyone else about this stuff.

I was brave when the doctor told me I need an operation, but when I went to bed later, I just cried. I can't remember what it's like not to ever worry about health or operations. I can't remember what it's like not to wonder if I will be able to understand people. Every time I meet someone, I pray that I will be able to lipread them. Often I can, but sometimes I can't.

Everything is hard work.

God knows

That operation I mentioned last time went fine, and I've been doing more speaking, about the Bible as well as my testimony. I spoke at a church women's group last week, and I couldn't believe it when they told me what they wanted me to speak about. Psalm 139. The psalm I don't like and try not to think about! But I can't not think about it if I have to speak about it, can I?

It went OK, but here's the bit I did *not* speak about – and I'm only telling you this, not anyone else:

'You made my whole being. You formed me in my mother's body.
I praise you because you made me in an amazing and wonderful way.
What you have done is wonderful.
I know this very well.
You saw my bones being formed as I took shape in my mother's body.
When I was put together there, you saw my body as it was formed.
All the days planned for me were written in your book before I was one day old.'

God knew what my days would be like. God knew I had tumours, even before I was born. That's really hard, and it's why I didn't speak about that bit.

But now I think about it, isn't it better that God knows than that he doesn't? Even if it's hard sometimes?

#everydayrainbows: God

Gaps

So many gaps. I've just been reading this diary through, and it's all gaps. Hearing in left ear taken away? Gap. Smile taken away? Gap. Hearing, walking, blinking, eating taken away? Gap, gap,

gap, gap. But God's been with me all the way. It's like he's been there to fill the gaps. I definitely feel closer to him.

Who's that?

My friend Rachel came over today and saw, hanging by the stairs, a photo of my family. It was taken ages ago, before she knew me. Rachel looked at the photo, then asked me who the person wearing green was. It was me! She didn't recognize me. My own friend didn't recognize me.

I forget that some people didn't know me before all the damage. I don't like being reminded and I try not to look at the photo, but I had to tell Rachel it was me wearing green. I'm so damaged now, she didn't even recognize me. Great.

But she looked at the photo and then at me and said, 'I prefer you now because that's how I know you.'

#everydayrainbows: I didn't think anyone would prefer me now

Grace

I read, in 2 Corinthians 12, about grace. Grace is when God helps us do and be things we couldn't do or be on our own. Paul wrote this bit in the

Bible about grace. Paul had something really hard going on in his life, and he wrote:

> 'I begged the Lord three times to take this problem away from me. But the Lord said to me, "My grace is enough for you. When you are weak, then my power is made perfect in you."'

I need to learn about grace.

God has given me so much grace already; I know I couldn't live my life without God helping me. I'm weaker than ever. There is so much I can't do now. But if I could still do those things, maybe I wouldn't have learned about grace?

I need more grace.

It's hard to be weak all the time, but I think Paul is right, don't you? The more I rely on God, the stronger I am. Every time I say to God 'I can't do this' – and I say it a *lot*, at least once a day – it's like he replies, 'No, *but we* can.' And he's right.

#everydayrainbows: God

Runaway horse

I've been thinking more about grace. I think it means God's grace is enough to help me each day.

When I was 6, I went to a fair with my grandparents. One of the things to do there was have a ride on a horse, just up and down the field. The horse was big but I felt safe sitting on it because someone led it, until halfway up the field it suddenly reared up on its back legs. I managed not to fall off, but then it pulled its reins from the man leading it and galloped away across the field. I was still on its back, screaming. I was terrified!

Eventually, the man caught it and led it back to where it started. I just wanted to get off, but he said I needed to go for a ride otherwise I would always be scared to go on a horse. So I did. And he was right: I'm not scared to go on horses now.

I think maybe it's a bit like that with grace. Remember that time when God told me to let go of what I thought my life would be – university, teaching, children? Life was scary and I didn't want to go on. I wanted life to stop so I could get off. But God told me to get back on.

'My grace is enough for you.'

Grace is definitely #everydayrainbows. To be honest, life is still scary sometimes. I know I have more tumours in my body. It's hard not being able to hear. I need grace to help me through.

#everydayrainbows: grace

Live the life we have

Sometimes I wish I was sitting on those blue plastic chairs in my leotard again, even though I felt stupid. Back then I had never even seen a brain scan, let alone looked at tumours in my own head. At least I could walk properly, and run, and all the rest I can't do now. It had never crossed my mind I would lose my hearing. OK, be deaf. There. I said it.

But you know what? I know that my redeemer liveth. I do. My life has changed, but God never changes. He's always there. Sometimes I wish my life was different, but I'd rather have this life with God, than any other life without him.

Everyone is different. We all just need to try to live the life we have. And my life does have rainbows in it.

When people went off to university and I didn't, I told myself not to compare, because it would only make me sad. I still try not to compare myself with other people. Like that bit in the Bible, in John 21, when one of Jesus' disciples, called Peter, asks Jesus, 'What about John? Is he getting a better life than me?' and Jesus says, 'Don't compare yourself with him, Peter; you just follow me.'

That means, don't keep wishing you were other people, just concentrate on following Jesus. It's one of my favourite bits in the Bible.

#everydayrainbows: follow Jesus

Everyday rainbows

I'm going to stop writing this diary now. I hope Mum doesn't mind! But I think I've kept my promise to her that I'd write it.

Thanks for reading it; I know I said it's a secret, but I'm glad you read it. It helped me feel less alone.

When I started writing it, I could hear, but now I can't. I could smile, but now I can't. I could run, but now I can't.

I'm not the same person, but do you know what? I am the same deep down. If this diary taught me anything, it's that whatever happens, I'm safe with God. I mean safe deep down. He never lets go of me.

This diary has taught me about #everydayrainbows, too. Finding something good in every day, even if I'm having a rubbish day. Maybe you can look for #everydayrainbows, too?

Living is Christ

I really miss music, but I have lots of it in my memory. I call it my music-memory. I can still sing in tune. I sing out loud in the shower. Ha, be glad you don't live in my house! Mostly, I just sing in my head, but I still sing. A lot of the time, I sing songs about Jesus. They remind me that the most important thing in life is knowing him.

Living is Christ . . . #everydayrainbows

Reflective Questions

- What's the most important thing in your life?

  Why?

  Is this good or bad?

- If you had to choose, would you rather be blind or deaf?

  Why?

  How do you think you would feel?

  What do you think you would miss the most?

- Why might people not have wanted Emily to do Sunday school after she was deaf? **Subtitles** (p. 74).

- Why might Emily's family have found her situation difficult?

  How do you think you might feel if Emily was your sister?

- Why might it have been difficult for Emily to choose to have surgery? **Laughing** (p. 149).

- Which do you think is worse: losing hearing, or losing the use of a facial nerve? **Deaf** (p. 27).

  Why?

  How do you think you would feel?

  What do you think you would miss the most?

- Do you know anyone who has a disability?

  If not, think about someone you may have seen who has a disability/is different from you.

  Has Emily's story changed the way you think about them? If so, how?

- Eric Liddell put God first when he ran, and ran for the glory of God. He was good at running and his running made God happy. **Chariots of Fire** (p. 174).

  What are you good at?

  If you believe in God, do you put him first/use your gifts for him?

- Do you know what Emily means by God's Great Big Peace? **Great Big Peace** (p. 177).

  Can you think of a situation when you felt Great Big Peace (a time when you felt peace even if you were nervous or scared)?

- Is there something you would like God's grace to help you with? You can use your own words to talk to God, or you could use the prayer below. Remember, God's grace is what he gives us to help us do and be things we can't do on our own. **Grace** and **Runaway horse** (pp. 183, 184).

Prayer

Hello God,
Thank you that I can talk to you.
Talking to you is definitely a rainbow.
I'm glad I know about Great Big Peace,
but sometimes things are still difficult.
Is it OK to tell you that, just like Emily does?
I think it is. I can talk to you about anything.
I'm finding ……………………… hard at the moment.
I need your grace to help me.
Please will you help me?
Thank you.
Amen

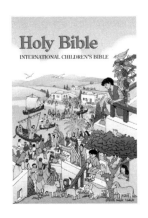

ICB

International Children's Bible

The *International Children's Bible* is not an adult Bible especially packaged for children. It has specifically been translated directly from the Hebrew and Greek texts into English so that it can be read and understood by children between the ages of 6 and 12.

The *ICB* is a full text Bible that every child will be delighted to own. With guidance, daily Bible reading can easily become a pleasurable habit that will last a lifetime.

Features include:
• Large, easy to read type in two columns
• Simple footnotes explain names, customs and phrases
• 32 full colour illustrations with multi-cultural images
• A dictionary helps explains difficult words and phrases
• Presentation page
• Colour maps
• Ribbon marker

With simpler language and extra notes and helps, the *ICB* is the perfect Bible for a child who is ready to move on from a picture Bible to a full text Bible.

978-0-85009-901-0

God's Amazing Plan Bible

The price he paid to win your love

Amy Parker

God's Amazing Plan Bible seeks to emphasise the ways God works to bring about salvation; from choosing His people and saving them from slavery to establishing them as a nation and finally, at the right time, sending His Son Jesus Christ, the ultimate saviour.

Each story ends with key Bible verses for the reader to reflect on. These verses, taken as a whole, are like beads on a string, connecting the Bible storybook to the biblical text while also connecting the reader to the main message, theme, or idea of each story, expressed in the Bible's own words.

With easy to read language and engaging colour illustrations, this is perfect for 8-12 year olds to understanding the overall themes of the Bible.

978-1-78893-110-6

The Illustrated Children's Bible

Rhona Davies

A beautifully illustrated Bible that is perfect for children who are ready to move on from their first Bible.

This new Bible contains over fifty stories that are retold and vibrantly illustrated in a way that will appeal to children in Key Stage 2. It is perfect for children who can now read and engage with the Bible for themselves, and are ready to dig a little deeper into the details of the Biblical stories.

The Illustrated Children's Bible is perfect for parents looking to move beyond a first bible. A presentation page is also included that helps makes this a perfect gift for a special occasion or a First Communion.

978-1-78893-007-9

BibleForce

The first heroes Bible

Do you know the true heroes of the Bible?

Dive into the action and adventure of the Bible! *BibleForce* retells the Scriptures using stunning art and a fast-paced narrative that children can understand. Following the events of the Bible in chronological order, the simple, straight-forward retelling of the scripture will keep children totally captivated. You and your child can read about Bible heroes together, and the text is simple enough for young ones to read on their own.

BibleForce includes over 150 of the most epic stories in the Bible, retold in a dramatic art style which brings characters to life. Hero profiles for key characters help children deepen their understanding and maps and a timeline help set the scene for the stories.

978-1-78893-004-8

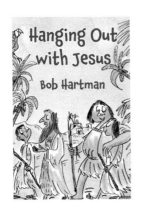

Hanging Out with Jesus

Adventures with my best mates

Bob Hartman

Big Bart, Tommo and me, Pip. Three guys on a three-year adventure, hanging out with Jesus, finding out what he's up to. Not exactly the best known of the twelve disciples, but we're on the edge of the action – out of the limelight, where there is plenty of partying, messing about and time to make idiots of ourselves.

We're best mates. And Jesus' mates, too. Every day with Jesus is so special, I've written the stories down; stories you'll find in the Bible if you take a look. Well, sort of, because everything is just a little bit different when you're hanging out with us.

978-1-78893-029-1

Hanging Out with Jesus Again
Bob Hartman
978-1-78893-119-9

Prayers and Answered Prayers

Filled with questions and creative prompts, *Prayers and Answered Prayers* is a perfect book for kids to store their prayers and record the things they're thankful for.

Inside the vinyl jacket, readers will find two postcard-shaped books with stunning, glittery covers. The books contain related content: one book to record your prayers and another to record your blessings!

The perfect book for tweens who love recording their prayers, blessings and much more!

978-1-86024-975-4

Do consider inviting Emily to speak at your church, event or school.

Emily has a powerful testimony, which she regularly shares. She longs for people to realise who God has made them to be and that, no matter what happens in life, value comes through having an identity rooted in Christ.

Emily is a regular speaker and is passionate about making the Bible relevant and accessible to people today.

Contact details:
Twitter: @EmilyOwenAuthor
Facebook: @EmilyOwenAuthor
www.emily-owen.co.uk

30 Days with . . . Emily Owen

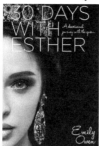

30 Days with Esther
A devotional journey with
the queen
978-1-78078-448-9

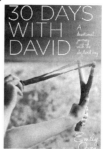

30 Days with David
A devotional journey with
the shepherd boy
978-1-78078-449-6

30 Days with Mary
A devotional journey with
the mother of Jesus
978-1-86024-935-8

30 Days with Elijah
A devotional journey with
the prophet
978-1-86024-937-2

30 Days with Ruth
A devotional journey with
the loyal widow
978-1-78893-179-3

30 Days with John
A devotional journey with
the disciple
978-1-86024-936-5

The Power of Seven

49 devotional reflections
7 biblical themes
Genesis to Revelation

Emily Owen

Written in Emily Owen's unique, poetic style, this series of forty-nine devotions on seven biblical themes will inspire and gently steer you into a closer walk with Jesus.

Emily seamlessly weaves together reflections, prayers, personal stories and the encouraging 'voice' of God. Enjoy the world he gave you and stand together with him, with these seven themes as your guide: Creation, God *Is*, The Lord is My Shepherd, I AM, Echoes from the Cross, Add to Faith and Revelation Churches.

Be refreshed as you allow these powerful, thoughtful and imaginative reflections to point you to Jesus.

978-1-78078-990-3

God's Calling Cards

*Personal reminders of his
presence with us*

Emily Owen

What does it mean to be called – or to hear the call of God?

Using biblical examples and moving personal testimony, Emily Owen
invites us to lean in to listen to God, to expect him to speak and,
ultimately, to be close enough to hear and recognize his voice.

This devotional gently encourages us to personally encounter the
God who loves us and to look out for God's calling cards in our lives.

978-1-78893-025-3

Authentic

We trust you enjoyed reading this book from Authentic. If you want to be informed of any new titles from this author and other releases you can sign up to the Authentic newsletter by scanning below:

Online:
authenticmedia.co.uk

Follow us: